Stream Safety & Fly Fishing

Stream Safety & Fly Fishing

G. R. Murphy

**MOUNTAIN ARBOR
PRESS** *a Division of BookLogix*
Alpharetta, Georgia

Although the author and publisher have made every effort to ensure that the information in this book was correct at the time of first publication, the author and publisher do not assume and hereby disclaim any liability to any party for any loss, damage, or disruption caused by errors or omissions, whether such errors or omissions result from negligence, accident, or any other cause.

Copyright © 2025 by G. R. Murphy

All rights reserved. No part of this book may be reproduced or transmitted in any form or by any means, electronic or mechanical, including photocopying, recording, or any information storage and retrieval system, without permission in writing from the author.

ISBN: 978-1-6653-0949-3 - Paperback
eISBN: 978-1-6653-0950-9 - eBook

These ISBNs are the property of Mountain Arbor Press (a Division of BookLogix) for the express purpose of sales and distribution of this title. The content of this book is the property of the copyright holder only. Mountain Arbor Press does not hold any ownership of the content of this book and is not liable in any way for the materials contained within. The views and opinions expressed in this book are the property of the Author/Copyright holder, and do not necessarily reflect those of Mountain Arbor Press/BookLogix.

Library of Congress Control Number: 2025909735

∞This paper meets the requirements of ANSI/NISO Z39.48-1992 (Permanence of Paper)

All photos provided by G. R. Murphy

0 6 2 4 2 5

I dedicate this book to my wife. She has supported me in my fly-fishing ventures. She doesn't have a lot of interest in fly fishing but she goes with me anyway. She's the one who encouraged me to get back into fishing after a long absence, and I am glad she did.

Contents

Introduction ix

Chapter 1	Fly Fishing 101	1
Chapter 2	Hooked	5
Chapter 3	Location, Location, Location	9
Chapter 4	First Aid Kits and Other Medical Need-to-Knows	13
Chapter 5	Follow the Signs	19
Chapter 6	Wading Safely	23
Chapter 7	Safety Devices	37
Chapter 8	Dam-Controlled Rivers	41
Chapter 9	Fishing Close to Waterfalls	45
Chapter 10	Wildlife Encounters	49
Chapter 11	Farm Animals, Pets, and Unattended Children	63
Chapter 12	The Weather	67
Chapter 13	Personal Flotation Device	75
Chapter 14	Dress for the Weather	79
Chapter 15	Fishing with a Buddy	83
Chapter 16	Hydration	87
Chapter 17	Things to Watch Out for While on the Stream	91
Chapter 18	When Nature Calls	97
Chapter 19	Hiking into the Backwoods, to a Stream	101
Chapter 20	Have a Good Knife	107

Chapter 21	Carrying a Firearm While Fishing	111
Chapter 22	Communication	115
Chapter 23	"Hey, What Is That Guy Doing in the Water?"	119
Chapter 24	Debris and Obstacles in the Water	123
Chapter 25	Taking Out the Trash	127
Chapter 26	Get Your Mind Right	131
Chapter 27	In Closing	137

Acknowledgments   139

Introduction

Stream safety seems to be something most people never even think about, especially when you go out for a day of fly fishing. You see, fly fishing is a bit different because it's usually done in more remote areas. Sometimes accessibility to these areas can be limited or challenging as well. Remember, if a space or location is hard to get into, it will also be hard to get out of. Now, if you get injured while you are back there—then escape is going to become even more complicated.

I'm sure when you think about fly fishing, *safety* is not the first concern that comes to mind. Well, honestly, it is really something that should be considered. Believe it or not, people *do* get injured while fly fishing, and unfortunately, a few people have lost their lives, usually due to drowning. This can be avoided if you understand stream safety.

I have been what I call an "Adventure Fisherman" all my life—meaning I would hike into a lot of places to fish. And I'm talking about places "Bigfoot" is scared to go!

How do I know this, you ask? Well, because I never saw him in any of those places, of course! I will admit in my younger days I never really thought about getting injured or any risks. I never really considered what I was going to do if I got hurt and couldn't get out under my own power. I simply never gave it a single thought. In a situation like this, I'm sure the first thing that you think is to call someone on your cell phone. Well, believe it or not, back in the '80s, cell phones did not exist. When they started coming out, they were usually "bag" or "brick" phones, and the reception was terrible. *Ah, the '80s.* I remember seeing guys carrying around a "brick phone" in nightclubs, trying to impress someone. This was back in the days when you had to walk to school, and it was uphill . . . both ways, and it snowed year-round!

Anyway, due to my chosen occupation, advancing years, and personal experiences, I have become more aware of these things, and you should too.

So, you may be wondering why and how I came up with the idea of writing a book on safety and fly fishing. I have spent my life as an outdoor enthusiast. Also, for thirty-three years of my life, I was a professional firefighter, as well as an emergency medical technician (EMT).

During my years of being a firefighter/EMT, I had a lot of opportunities for all types of training. As we progressed and grew as a department, the spectrum of our training started to expand into different areas other than fighting fire and EMS. Some of the more unusual training we got into was wilderness-type rescue situations, such as "land search" and "water rescue." The most enjoyable, and the one that stands out the most is Swiftwater Rescue Technician. These classes gave me a new respect for moving water. To be totally honest, I had a personal interest in this class because at the time, I was really into whitewater rafting. However, I never thought this training would have such an impact on my life and especially my fishing habit. Yes, there were times I did have to use that training as well.

So, with all that being said, I have drawn on my experience as a firefighter/EMT, my Swiftwater Rescue Technician training, and the many years I've spent as an outdoor enthusiast to put this book together.

Also, in an effort to keep you from becoming bored and losing interest in the book, I have tried to keep the chapters short and even added in some humor to hopefully keep things moving. Hopefully, you will get a laugh or two out of it, but most of all, I hope you learn some useful information.

One last thing before you begin—this book mainly discusses situations related to fishing freshwater streams in wooded and/or remote areas. I do realize the sport of fly fishing extends beyond these areas, such as coastal and saltwater areas. But my experience is mostly in the terrain mentioned above.

And before you think this book is a waste of time, because none of this has ever happened to you or anyone you know, please remember this, something I heard a lot of people say when I would arrive on the scene of a call when I was a firefighter was, "This kind of thing has never happened to me."

Chapter 1

Fly Fishing 101

You get up in the morning and load up your vehicle with all your equipment to spend the day out on the water, fly fishing. You have got your waders, rods and reels, enough flies to last the next year—*or twelve*—a net, and maybe a wading staff—which everyone should use, as it is a safety device to help with your balance.

You're all set! Right?

How about a first aid kit? You do have one of those, don't you? If you do, would you know how to use it if you had to? Have you had any type of first aid training? When you were in a scout troop, maybe?

Okay, let's say you are going to your "top secret" fishing hole. You know—the one only *you* know about. The one you have to hike back to? Nobody ever goes back there because it's so difficult to get to. Now, think about this . . .

What if something happens to you while you're back there? Let's say you have a medical emergency while you're back there in the secret hole—*that only you know about.*

Are you going to be able to get out under your own power? Maybe you decided to bring along your buddy. Is your buddy going to be able to help you get out of the secret hole in an emergency? Do you have cell service? And even if you do have service, are you going to be able to tell the 911 Telecommunicator your location?

Let's throw another scenario out there. You are fishing down in the bottom of a gorge or a canyon. Has it ever crossed your mind how most of these places were formed?

Water. It is one of the most powerful forces on earth. Now, this powerful water that created these landmarks happened several million years ago, but it still may be susceptible to flooding.

If you have a boat, there are classes you can take on boater safety. If you hunt, there are classes on hunting and gun safety, but if you want to go buy some waders and walk around in a stream of moving water in the middle of nowhere—have at it, have fun!

Now, let's head out in the middle of nowhere and go walk around in a stream full of moss-covered, slippery rocks and logs. Let's not forget the sandy bottoms—and I use that term *bottom* loosely. Some stream bottoms can fool you, meaning it could be a false bottom where a bunch of sand has *collected* and can act almost like quicksand. Remember the old *Tarzan* movies? He was a pro at getting out of that stuff, but that was the movies, this is real life.

Anyway, this isn't a book to scare you off from fly fishing. It's just to give you some tools that will make you more aware of your surroundings while you are out there. With the exception of fishing in a lake or pond, it seems the majority of us are going to be fishing in moving water of some type, such as a creek or river which may be fast or slow, but it's still moving. Streams of all types seem to experience cycles. High water, low water, fast-moving or slow-moving, continually changing. Some over years, some over days. And in some cases, over minutes. You must remember moving water is one of the most powerful natural forces on Earth and can be unpredictable. The key term here is, "moving" so you should always remember, the water never gets tired, but you will.

Chapter 2

Hooked

Okay, it's going to happen sooner or later. You are going to be impaled by a hook. It is probably one of the most common injuries any fisherman experiences. This is the number one reason why I use barbless hooks. Simply because they come out a heck-of-a lot easier. Whether it be in a fish's mouth or your finger (*or some other body part,* I'm just saying). I can't tell you how many times I have stabbed myself in the finger while I was trying a new fly, especially those tiny ones. Other times, you may have just landed a fish, and while it is still in the net, the fish decides he does not like the taste of the fly, so it decides to shake its head, throwing the hook, and it ends up impaling you in the hand.

You may be fishing near someone who isn't careful, or they may not cast the best line, and they smack you in the head with a fly on a back cast or something. These, among many others, are good reasons to fish with barbless hooks. Oh, and it's less harmful to the fish as well.

Now if you tie your own flies, you can buy barbless hooks. Or you can simply smash the barb before you start tying it and stab yourself in the finger or thumb. This is also a good idea because if you were to drop it on the floor, you know someone is going to find it probably with their bare feet. Again, I say, the barbless comes out a lot easier, and maybe you'll even avoid a trip to the emergency room.

Whether you go barbless or not, it is still a good idea to know how to remove a barbed hook. I am not going to tell you how to remove hooks because with us now having the World Wide Web at our fingertips, I am sure there are plenty of videos online on how to remove a hook from flesh. Just remember alcohol should be used as an antiseptic, not as a painkiller.

On that note, what do you do if you find a lost or discarded fly? Usually, if I find a lost fly and it's in decent shape, I may try to keep it and use it again. But if it's a mess, I will take it with me to properly dispose of it later.

Speaking of hooks, in some places I have fished, I've seen these things called a "Flybrary."

You may occasionally find these in different spots around or near fishing access points, such as on a bridge or a sign. It's almost a place to donate a fly. That's always a good place to put one if the fly isn't in bad shape or you can always leave a couple for the next person.

Now, while we are on the subject of flying hooks, we need to talk about sunglasses. Sunglasses are pretty much a requirement for fishing, but they can have another use, and that is eye protection from an erratic fly on a bad cast. To keep the fly, strike indicator, or split shot hitting you in the eye and injuring you, or someone else.

It's always good to have sunglasses for eye protection from UV rays, irritating bugs, and flying hooks, as well as being able to spot a few fish.

After doing some research to try and find out if there was a national statistic on hook removal in hospitals, I really didn't find a number nationwide, but I did find one hospital that started keeping records on this type of injury in 1996. Since then, the record has risen up to 1,191 hooks removed.

Also, this is a good reason to keep a tube of some type of antiseptic in your first aid kit. Especially if you have already caught a fish or two with that particular hook. You don't want to get an infection. Again, an *antiseptic, not* a pain killer. Besides, you don't need anything to interfere with fishing time!

Chapter 3

Location, Location, Location

A common reference in the real estate business is "Location, Location, Location." Well, this could go for the fishing game as well. We all want to know where the fish are. Sometimes that location isn't the most convenient place to get to, but when you get there, and the fish are biting, it's worth the trek. Now, say a thunderstorm comes up all of a sudden and you need to get out of there in a hurry and you need to get back to your vehicle. You should remember, you are carrying a nine-foot fly rod, also known as a lightning rod in a thunderstorm.

This is one thing about location. Do you have cell service? If not, do you know how far you are going to have to go to get a good signal—and in what direction? If you did for some reason have an emergency, could you tell the 911 Telecommunicator your location? Yes, a lot of emergency services can lock onto your signal and find your location, but what if they can't? That's why it's a good thing to be familiar with the area. Out in some rural areas, addresses aren't always easy to find. So, look for landmarks as you get to where you are going. Maybe a little church or store, or an intersection if they have the road names on them. Once they dispatch the emergency vehicle, then they have to find you. in my experience, rural areas are notorious for not having house numbers or addresses in plain sight, making it almost impossible to find the correct location in an emergency.

If you're able to get to your vehicle, and you have cell service, tell them the make and model of your car, and stay where you are. The emergency vehicle that is responding will be looking for the location you provided. Now, let's say you're driving a white pickup. Be a bit more descriptive about it. Does it have a camper top on it, or do you have some kind of stickers on the back window? Be as specific as possible.

Another option is your key fob. Today, most of us are driving vehicles that come with key fobs, and most of them have an "emergency" button on them, which causes the horn to blow and the lights to flash repeatedly. I'm sure you have seen this before when someone in a parking lot pushes the wrong button and announces their presence. Or you can simply turn on your four-way flashers.

Remember, if you fish in an area on a regular basis, you should begin to remember landmarks for this reason. Another thing you can do is find out where the closest fire station, rescue squad, or ranger station may be. Also, pay attention to where your cell service gets weak or drops out completely. This way you will have an idea of where your closest area with service is in the event of an emergency.

Now, before you go fishing it will be in your best interest to find the closest teenager and ask them to make sure your "location share" feature on your cell phone is turned on. Today, with all the technology, most mobile phones have "location share" services. One good thing about these services is they constantly monitor your location. If you were to get out of the service area, it should remember your last reported location, so if nothing else, it will get you in the neighborhood, so to speak. Remember, it never hurts to do things the old-fashioned way and tell someone where you are going and what time you will be back.

There are actually companies building devices just for the purpose of being able to locate a person that may be out of cell phone range. One is a Personal Locator Beacon or PLB, and another is the Satellite Emergency Notification Device or SEND. There will be a bit more information on this technology later on in the book.

Now, time is of the essence if you experience an emergency medical situation. You may be in a community that has a volunteer fire department or rescue squad. But keep in mind, some of these stations may not be "manned" all the time, or they may have one or two paid members on duty—it just depends on the community. Depending on the situation, when you call 911, they send out the page to *all* volunteers. Those that are available will respond, but it may be from their home or wherever they are at that time. They may show up in some type of emergency apparatus such as a fire truck or an ambulance or it may be in their personal vehicle. It just depends on the situation. Regardless, *someone* will show up.

Here's a few things to note about volunteers at fire departments and rescue squads. The key word here is *volunteer*. Folks, the volunteers do these out of a commitment to their community. They spend time away from their homes and their families for training and other department requirements. Some of the places you fish may be very rural and don't have the tax base to support hiring personnel. So that's why they might see someone in their personal vehicle. When you call 911 in one of these communities, they are most likely going to be a volunteer with the local fire department or rescue squad.

If you have never been one of these volunteers or don't know anyone who has, these people do this on their own dime. Meaning they respond to calls in their private vehicle they paid for and, of course, pay for the gas in it. A lot of them have to pay for their own training outside of what their department provides. If they get a call at three in the afternoon, or three in the morning, they are going to do whatever they can to get there, again, usually on their own dime. So, if you ever find yourself in need of one of these volunteers, be very gracious.

Chapter 4

First Aid Kits and Other Medical Need-to-Knows

Do you have a first aid kit, and do you know how to use it? Do you even know what's in it? There are companies out there that build fairly generic first aid kits, and then there are some companies that build more specialized kits. If you decide to buy yourself one, it's a good idea to know everything inside, and how to use it. Furthermore, if you're looking to fish somewhere remotely, and you've never had any training in first aid, it's probably a good idea to pursue some education in this area.

Some people buy a first aid kit, throw it in their car, and leave it there. That's fine, but you must remember, there might be some things in the kit that are temperature sensitive, so it's a good idea to take it out every once in a while, to check it out. For that matter, if you have one at home, it's a good idea to check it occasionally because there may be something in there with an expiration date or a limited shelf life that needs to be replaced. Believe me, you do not want to find this out when it's too late! Pro tip—if there is something in there with an expiration, I put a reminder on my phone. Folks, if I can figure out how to do that then you shouldn't have a problem. Again, if you have problems doing this, find a teenager to take care of it for you.

Now let's talk about medical issues. Do you have any? Do you have a buddy you fish with on a regular basis? Do *they* have some kind of medical issue? It's best that your friends know this, so if something happens and you require emergency medical assistance, your friend can tell the EMT's and paramedics if you are unable to explain. It's also a good idea to keep a list of medications you take on a regular basis, to give to the first responders. Believe me, this will be a tremendous help to them.

Okay, if you are new to fishing, there are people called guides. You pay a guide to lead—or *guide* you on this venture. So, you should be sure and tell them if you need to eat at a certain time, or you have to take your meds at a certain time. If you go on a full-day trip with a guide and they provide food, make sure to tell them if you have any certain dietary needs. I'm sure they will do what they can to accommodate you. My experience with guides has always been good, but there will be those that may leave you lacking. Before you hire a guide, do your research before you spend any money.

Okay, here is a scenario for you. You are a heart patient, meaning you have had a heart attack in the past or your doctor has told you that you are a candidate to have one. Maybe you had a heart attack a few years ago, and now you have to take Nitroglycerin pill, as needed. Let's say you are on a guided trip, you've just been hooked into a massive brown trout, and it took you several minutes to land it. Once you've reeled him in, took pictures, and all the excitement is beginning to calm, you start to feel a slight discomfort in your chest, a radiating pain in your left arm. Are you going to be macho and not say anything about it? Maybe you feel a little embarrassed because you don't want the guide to see you take one of your pills. Chances are the guide is not going to recognize these signs.

But that leads us to our next medical precaution. Do you know how to perform Cardiopulmonary resuscitation? More commonly known as CPR—this method saves lives! It is most effective when started immediately if cardiac arrest is witnessed. If you don't know how to perform CPR, it would be in your best interest to learn. There are plenty of resources online to find classes.

Let's talk about another situation—hypothermia. Hypothermia is loosely defined as your core temperature cooling down rapidly. For this reason, it is good to carry a towel and some extra clothes just in case you do take an unexpected dip in the water— especially on a cold day. This too could save your life. If you were to take that unexpected bath, you would need to get out of all the wet clothes, dry off, and get somewhere to get your core temperature to warm back up. I'm not going to go in great detail about this, because there is a lot better information on the World Wide Web that can explain it better than I can.

Speaking of hypothermia, remember the term "Killer Cotton." This is a term used by a lot of hikers and backpackers. The reason being cotton tends to absorb moisture—such as perspiration— and hold it, so wearing cotton while wading may not be the best idea, in the event you do fall in the water. What you need is a fabric that repels moisture like polypropylene, wool, or some other wicking fiber. Regardless of what type of material you are wearing, if you do go in the water, you need to get the wet stuff off, then dry off and get somewhere warm and get your core temp back up to normal.

Anaphylactic shock. If you are allergic to insect bites, or stings, or even have food allergies, then you should know what this is. Basically, it's what happens to people that have certain allergies to food and/or insect bites, which causes a severe allergic reaction. If you are susceptible to this, I strongly suggest you obtain an EpiPen and keep it close by at all times. Being an EMT, I have had to use these on patients before and I have seen what they can do. They save lives! Remember this, we are going to go over insects later on in this book.

Now, antiseptic. A little of this can go a long way. I know what you are thinking, *"Why in the world would I need this?"* Well, funny you should ask. It doesn't matter how clean you think the water is. It may be crystal clear and cool as a cucumber, but that does not mean it's completely clean. So, it is a good idea to have some type of antiseptic on hand. If for some reason you end up with a hook in your hand, now you may have caught a few fish on this hook, there is no telling what may be on that hook and now you may have just introduced it into your bloodstream. Chances are very unlikely this will happen but it's always better to be safe than sorry.

If you have never had any first aid training, it probably wouldn't hurt to sign up for a class somewhere. First aid and CPR training are very good to have. There are a number of online classes you can sign up for, or if you prefer in-person training, you may be able to find something locally through a community college. Folks, this would be time well spent for this training. If you just had to use it one time, it would pay off.

If you have a buddy, or a group you fish with, then maybe you all could take the class together, that way you can practice together, and some people are more comfortable learning as a group especially since they all know each other. With that being said, it wouldn't hurt for all of you to get together occasionally to run some practice scenarios and keep each other sharp.

From my experience as an EMT, I can tell you that the biggest problem in a medical situation is denial. You don't want to be several miles from a hospital when you start feeling bad, and play it off, claiming it's just heartburn or gas from a breakfast burrito you ate that morning. Meanwhile, you have chewed up half of a bottle of antacids with no relief. It's past time to go for help. Get help as soon as possible and get checked out by a medical professional.

Another item to consider is some type of "medic alert" or medical information tag. Now this can be in the form of a bracelet, necklace or a patch. I have even seen where some people have them in the form of a tattoo. There are all types of items with this info on them and they can be a tremendous help in emergency situations. Also, this is something that will be handy for everyday wear.

Chapter 5

Follow the Signs

Due to over-development and some careless fisherman, sooner or later, you are going to run across posted property. You may fish one area of a stream for years, then go back one day and see NO TRESPASSING signs everywhere, or even purple paint on trees or fence posts. This is the landowner's right. It may be the same landowner who has owned it for years, or it may be a new landowner. Laws on this may vary from state to state. It's best you check with the local law enforcement agency to find out what the laws are in that area.

If landowners are gracious enough to let people fish on their property, please be courteous while you are there. Don't be too loud, and please don't leave trash on their property. If the property owner happens to be out there, be sure and thank them for allowing you to fish on their property. Believe me, I have spoken with landowner after landowner, and they all say the same thing—"People come in, drop their trash, and damage property." Mostly, just being disrespectful in general. Folks, look at it like the backpackers do: leave no trace. If you screw it up, then you screw it up for everybody.

Now, this is based off a true story. It's not my story, but a buddy of mine who would like to remain anonymous. If you are confronted by an angry landowner, just keep your cool and leave. Don't make any smart remarks or get in an argument with them. This can lead to a bad situation or even a physical confrontation. And when the law gets involved, it all goes downhill from there. You may get a free ride to the jailhouse, where you end up getting fingerprinted. They have a fancy photography studio where they will gladly take your picture. Then you get one phone call, and who are you going to call? If you call your significant other, you are going to have to hear it all the way home. If you call one of your buddies, then you are going to hear it from them and you know they are not going to be quiet about it. They are going to tell all the rest of your friends, so then they are going to bring it up every chance they get. Then just when you thought it couldn't get any worse, one of your buddies is looking at Facebook and happens to run across your mugshot on some site, and of course what do you think is going to happen then? They are going to share it with all of their friends, then it just snowballs from there. But wait, maybe somebody took their phone out and recorded it all! Then you end up on YouTube! But wait! You're sitting in church the following Sunday and the preacher brings it up in his sermon!

If that's not enough, next time you say something about going fishing, get ready because your significant other is going to have something smart to say like "Are you going fishing or going to jail? You know, we blew the kids' college fund on that attorney!" All of this to catch a fish! *Oh, the agony!*

Bottom line, if you see a sign that says NO TRESPASSING or purple paint on a tree or a fence post, then don't fish there—just go find somewhere else to fish and save yourself the aggravation.

Folks, this is just my personal opinion, a big contributor to the posted property thing is over-development of land. Some landowners may be getting "taxed out" of their property. Meaning, when they bought the property, there may have been nothing out there before civilization or development came to the place. These factors usually come with an increase in property taxes. So, the landowners get sick of paying high taxes, and they make the decision to sell out. Since the property value has gone up so much, the average person cannot afford the property. Then the developers come in with their deep pockets and have the resources to buy large tracts of land around a creek or stream and develop it into an exclusive community. And if you aren't a resident, you aren't allowed in.

A lot of good water is being lost to this type of thing. Every year when I return back to somewhere I have not fished in a while, I always see NO TRESPASSING signs that were not there the year before. I don't know if it will do any good, but you can contact your local representatives about this to see if they can do anything. Also, Trout Unlimited—an organization supporting trout habitat could be an avenue to explore.

Purple Paint Law: This is the real thing; it's not a joke. If you see where someone has painted a fence post or tree trunk with purple paint, this is pretty much representative of a NO TRESPASSING Sign. Not all states have adopted this yet, but regardless, if you encounter it somewhere, consider it a Sign. Off-limits.

Do these geese know that they are trespassing?

Chapter 6

Wading Safely

Okay, I'm going to say this right off the bat, wading can be a sensitive subject—known to cause big arguments at the breakfast table. There are all kinds of online discussions about it, and they can get pretty heated as well. It's comparable to an apples to oranges conversation. One thing you should always consider while wading through water, is if the water is moving too fast. If it is, you will want to stay out of it. If you have to fight the current while in the water, you are going to waste your energy and become tired. This is a bad situation to be in. Remember, *you* will get tired, but the water won't.

Folks, realistically, wading is probably the most dangerous

23

part of fly fishing. I mean, think about it. You are standing in water, trying to resist a current, and possibly debris continually drifting downstream. You really have no idea what is happening upstream, either, or anything in the water could be coming your way.

At times, you can be standing in frigid cold water, on an unstable bottom, with huge rocks all around you. Think about this, folks, one bad step and you can fall and hit your head on one of these rocks, get knocked unconscious, maybe even get a concussion, or even break a bone.

The worst-case scenario is drowning. One thing we will talk a lot about in this book is an "unstable bottom"—more on this later!

One thing to remember is that due to the constant current, stream beds are continuously changing, making them a dynamic environment. If you fish in the same stream long enough, you will see it. You see, a streambed is a dynamic environment because it is under constant change.

Now that we have that out of the way, let's talk about falling into the water while wearing waders. A lot of people have opinions about wearing waders and what happens if you fall in the water. Some say that when they fill with water, you are going to sink. Others say not. Folks, you must remember every situation is different, but regardless, the biggest thing you need to remember if you were to fall in the water is trying not to panic.

While you are out there you must remember to be aware of your surroundings. This is one thing I learned from taking Swiftwater Rescue courses. If you were to fall into fast-moving water and be swept away, try your best to remain calm, and whatever you do—*don't try to fight the current.* You will use too much energy and get tired quickly. Get on your back so you will be facing upward, put your arms straight out from your sides with your feet pointing downstream, and try to float. Pointing your feet downstream allows your feet and legs to work as a shock absorber, in case you were to hit an obstruction such as a large rock. While floating, watch for a slow place in the water, which is called an eddy. As soon as you see one, aim yourself in that direction. When you get close, flip over on your belly and swim into the eddy, then get out of the water and get the waders off. Do not try to swim against the current, you will only use up your precious energy and become tired. Remember, the current is pretty much perpetual, it does not tire, but you will.

Another thing that will come in handy if you fall in the water is a good wading belt. A snug wading belt will keep the majority of the water from going any further down into your waders, therefore adding less weight to your body. To add to that, some manufacturers even add a drawstring in the tops of their chest waders, where you can pull and snug the tops to help slow the intrusion of water during a submersion.

Also, one of the most underrated items to use while wading is a wading staff. A wading staff is much like a hiking staff, but it is used in the water. Basically, it creates a third point of contact and improves your balance. This is a plus while walking around on an uneven river bottom. You've got to remember, you are not walking down a concrete sidewalk in the city somewhere, you are walking across an unstable stream, the bottom of which may be full of all kinds of different things such as rocks, stones, sand, gravel, and countless others.

A wading staff can also work as a probe. You can use it to check the bottom, in front of you, and find out what you are about to step onto or into. It may be rocks or stone, or it may be sand, mud, or worse—a deep hole you could step in and go completely under the water. You will want to be very careful approaching because the drop-off may be very sudden, or it could collapse and cave in.

Another thing to remember is the wading staff does not have an age limit. Meaning you don't have to be a senior citizen to use one.

A wading staff can also help you when approaching the water. Once you get down to the bank, you can use the staff as a brace to help support your weight while you step into the water or while getting back out. They also work pretty well as hiking staff while you are on your way from point *A* to point *B*.

Folks, I will tell you this—if you decide to buy a wading staff, make sure it's a good one. Get one sturdy enough to support your weight. Before you buy, try it out, and make sure it's stable enough for you.

A lot of staffs are collapsible and come with a holster to store them in. Now, having them in the holster is fine for storage, but before you enter the water, the staff should be fully deployed. If you were to begin to fall while in the water and your wading staff is folded up in the holster, it's going to take several seconds to pull it out, and let it deploy, then get it into place, all before you take a bath. Plus, they tend to get stuck in the holster, so you'll have to use your other hand to hold the holster and the other to get it out

I must tell you; "Slip, Trip, and Fall" is not a matter of *if*—it is a matter of *when*. You may fish for years and never have a problem but believe me, the law of averages will catch up to you. There were a couple of times when I forgot my wading staff and was too lazy to go back and get it. Then later had regrets that I didn't go back.

Now, the next thing we're going to go over is a double-edge

sword. If you fish with a buddy or friends, this can be good or bad. If you fall, you will have someone around to help you if you need it. On the other hand—*hopefully you don't get hurt*—you are going to have to endure endless reenactments of how you fell, and what you did when you fell. We will go over more situations like this later on in the book.

Some people can fall gracefully. It almost looks like a ballet performance. Then there are the people who go into full-blown "Drama Queen" mode as they are falling. You know the ones; they wave their arms in the air as if they are trying to grasp something that is not there. Then facial expressions like that have nothing to do with improving balance. It's almost like they fall for fifteen minutes. Also, something else that never fails. It does not matter if anyone else is around or not. When the person finishes falling, they always have to look around to see if anyone witnessed it.

Folks, I know I am making a lot of fun of these situations, but they can also be a bad situation. Be careful out there.

Stream Safety & Fly Fishing

Let's talk about fishing upstream. We are always told to fish upstream simply because the fish are facing upstream, so when your bait is moving in the current going downstream, it's basically in the fish's line of sight. Well, that's one good reason to fish upstream. Another is to watch for debris. *Yes, I said debris.* Standing in a stream, the water is continually moving, carrying all kinds of things downstream. You see, water is pretty much continuous—it does not get tired. So, that tree that fell across the water, is eventually going to break down. And limbs and such are going to break off and head downstream. So, if one of these limbs is coming toward you while you're facing upstream, hopefully you will see it in time and move out of the way.

Have you ever waded under low-hanging tree limbs and around brush? This opens a whole new can of worms.

Let's say you are out on the river, and you see a few fish jump upriver about a hundred yards away, but there is only one way up there—to wade upriver to that spot. Let's say there is too much brush, it's too steep—or maybe you just don't want to get out of the water—so you move along, staying close to the bank, and on your way, you must duck down to go under a low hanging tree branch.

But you keep going. You've got to get up and try to catch those fish you spotted earlier. As you are moving upstream under the low-hanging branches, in your next step, your foot goes into a hole. At this moment, a good wading staff crosses your mind, but you don't have one because you think it will make you look old or something. *What do you do?* You quickly look up and see a tree branch above you, so you grab the limb, and now here are your options:

Option 1. Maybe you grab the limb, and everything is okay.

Option 2. You grab the limb and find out there are a few hooks in it from fly fishermen that suck at casting.

Option 3. You grab what you think is the limb, only to find out the limb is cold and has a scaly feel to it. If you haven't figured it out yet, it's a snake, and yes, snakes can climb trees. You will see a picture of that later in the book.

Option 4. You grab the limb, and you get a sudden stinging sensation. Which may be several different types of insects such as ants, hornets, wasps or some other type of biting or stinging insects.

Option 5. The tree limb is rotten. So, when you grab it, you hear a snap, and before you go in the water, the wading staff thing crosses your mind, again. I'm just saying . . .

Let's talk about waders. There are several different types of waders out there, and several different manufacturers. You can get chest-high waders, waist-high waders—also known as wading pants—and there are still a few companies that build "hippers" which basically come up to your crotch. The overall winner here seems to be the chest-high waders. Chest-high waders give you the most coverage obviously, because they will cover you probably almost up to your armpits. With that being said, they are going to give you the most insulation, since they also cover the torso where your vital organs are located. This will make a difference while fishing in colder weather. However, just because the waders come up high on you, doesn't mean you need to go into water that deep. Just remember, the more your body is exposed to the current, the greater the force of the current is going to be on you. This process will cause you to exert more energy, therefore you are going to become tired, then you may not have the energy to fight that monster Brown (also known as a brown trout) you just hooked into.

There are waders with built-in boots and then there are what they call "stocking" types that have no boots. You have to buy the boots separately. I think most people prefer the stocking type simply because when you slide your foot into the wading boot you get more ankle support, due to the laced-up boots. Whereas the "built-ins," you have a lot of room around your ankles. It's kind of like the difference between wearing slip-on boots, and a set of lace-up boots. You must remember, you are going to be walking around on an uneven surface, so ankle support is very important. Pro tip, the lace-up option is going to be the winner here. Remember, the idea is to enjoy your day fishing, so you don't want to end it suddenly because you turned your ankle. This is another reason to invest in a good wading staff. If, for some reason, you did turn your ankle, the wading staff will work almost as a crutch.

And it doesn't stop there. Be careful, as this subject has been known, to start an argument or two over breakfasts as well. Soles. For years the felt soles have been the choice of a lot of fishermen due to their ability to conform and stick to slimy moss-covered rocks, but from personal experience, they aren't worth a pinch of monkey poo-poo walking down a slick, grassy riverbank. More than once, I busted my *"bootius* maximus" going down a bank before falling in the water. Thankfully, nobody saw it, so it did not end up on YouTube.

Some states have or perhaps are in the process of outlawing felt soles, due to possible transfer of different diseases, such as "Whirling Disease" or Didymo. Now with the advantages of material technologies, some manufacturers are coming up with alternatives. Studded soles make a lot of difference, and I would've loved to have those on the old felt-bottom boots I used to wear. Personally, I have gone away from felt altogether, now using Vibram soles with studs.

While wading is important to understand, something you should always be mindful of is the bottom of whatever body of water you are in. You see, the bottom can change a lot in the same stream. One area may be gravel, sand in another area, or even mud.

Mud is a bad place because it's easy to get stuck in. Especially if it's soft and deep. Again, this is another good reason to have a wading staff, because you can probe the area with the staff and see the consistency of the bottom before you go and stick your big foot in there and get stuck.

Rocky, gravel bottoms can also present an issue as well. Rocks come in all sizes and shapes. Rocky bottoms can be somewhat unstable. You should never step on a rock thinking it's going to be stable, because it may move, throw you off balance, and end up in the water possibly resulting in an injury.

Sandy bottoms are another issue. Soft sand can be like mud. I had an experience while wading on a sandy bottom once. Not carrying a wading staff, I was making my way to what I thought was going to be a good place to fish, the next step I took on to the same sandy bottom I had been wading on, gave me a very unusual and frightening surprise. When I put my weight down on that foot, it didn't stop, it just kept sinking deeper in the sand. Once I realized what was happening, the first thing I thought of was, *what would* Tarzan *do?*

Okay, in all seriousness, the first thing I did was *not* panic. I was able to shift my weight back to my other foot and pull my foot out of the sand. Folks, I'm going to tell you right now that was a scary moment! Because of that incident, I don't step into water without a wading staff. Had I had one then, I may have been able to probe and find that spot before I stepped in it. Stupid moment, I had a wading staff, but I left it in my truck and was too lazy to go back and get it.

Let's talk a minute about "wet wading." For those of you that may not be familiar with the term wet wading, it's basically what it says. You bypass putting on the waders and just use your wading boots. Some people prefer to use "wading socks," which are made from neoprene. or they'll wear thick wool socks. This is, of course, for warm weather fishing. Wearing a set of regular waders in warm weather is going to be like wearing the sauna suits they had back in the '60s and '70s.

Some people will wear shorts while they're wet wading, and others wear long pants. I prefer to wear long pants simply for an extra layer of protection, and my legs don't see the sun enough to get a good tan, so I don't want to blind any fish. Anyway, the real reason for this is because I am always bumping into rocks, sticks, and whatever else in the water. So, wearing shorts, your legs are exposed to all of this and one little scratch or cut can lead to an infection. Years ago, you never heard of anything like this, but these days it seems to be more common. It's always good to have some type of antiseptic on hand for these situations. Hopefully, nothing like this will ever happen to you, but it is something to consider.

Now, let's talk about when you're ready to cross a stream. You should try and find the shallowest spot you can cross to, that way you have less current to deal with. A shallow area with a gravel bottom is a better choice. If you can't find an area like this to cross to—and you must cross in water—move at an upward angle, facing upstream, Beware of what is downstream because there could be strainers downstream, where if you fell and were swept away, you could be caught in one.

If you ever find yourself crossing a downed tree, or tree trunk, or what some people call a foot log, remember to be careful. If they have been there for a while, they may have developed some moss on them that could make them a bit slick. There is also a possibility of them not being stable. So, if you have balance issues you may want to reconsider this crossing.

Stepping on large stones to cross a creek that protrudes out of the water always looks good in the movies, but here in the real world, it does not always work that way. You see, stones do not always have a completely flat bottom, so they may look pretty stable in the water, then when you step over to it, put your foot on it, and it rocks . . . get it? It's rocks, stones! Okay, anyway, you find out it's not as stable as you thought it would be. This is something else you should always remember.

Some streams are full of rounded stones, almost like gravel. The problem here is they usually are not really packed down, meaning they are loose therefore unstable. Due to the shape of theses, they are almost "Ball Bearing" like. So, when you walk on them, they can roll under your feet causing an unstable situation, and you increase the chances of falling. Yet another good reason to have a wading staff. Have I said this already?

Something I always try to do while wading, is pick the point I want to get to, then figure my route—which may change depending on the structure of the bottom. I always try to look down to where my next step is going to be. Then place my foot there and make sure it's going to be stable before I take the next step. I know it sounds like a lot, but you will develop a rhythm after a bit and decrease your chances at taking a bath in the stream. Before taking a step, use your wading staff as a probe and also to support your weight.

Chapter 7

Safety Devices

A small flashlight of some type is always good to have. You never know when you will need one, and there are some really powerful, small flashlights out there now that shouldn't take up much room in your pack. Also, a headlamp can be something handy to have as well. It keeps your hands free.

While we are talking about lights, another type is some type of small emergency beacon. This is a flashing light to alert people of your location in an emergency situation. You don't have to go out and buy a really expensive beacon, you can generally find something that would be sufficient at a camping store or department store. Just make sure what you get is waterproof, and has a flashing option, and even better, try to find one that can be activated with one hand. Also, another battery-free option is a glow stick. They operate off of a chemical reaction, which is why they don't need batteries! When the two liquids inside the tube mix, they glow for several hours. However, they do have a shelf life, so you should check them periodically to make sure they haven't exceeded the expiration date.

So now that people can find you, we want them to be able to hear you as well. Another item to bring along is a whistle. According to my research, a whistle can be heard up to one mile away, maybe further, depending on the conditions. I also discovered most whistles operate between 500–5,000 Hz. Now to give you an idea, according to the research, 5,000 Hz is comparable to alarm and warning systems. The preferred type of whistle is what is known as a "pealess" whistle. It's obviously called this because it doesn't have the ball, or "pea," inside of it to give it that fluttering sound, but the main reason is, it has less chance of malfunctioning. These types of whistles are used extensively in Swiftwater Rescue operations. because they can be completely submerged in water, then one blow will expel the water out, and make a very shrill high-pitched sound to get someone's attention. To give you an idea, if you are out fishing somewhere you'll probably always hear another person elsewhere on the water hollering and making a lot of noise if they catch a big fish. So, yelling in an emergency situation may not always get others' attention, but a very shrill whistle is something you don't hear all the time, and should get some kind of attention—especially to someone with any type of rescue training. Anyone who hears something like this should investigate to find the source. But remember, don't play around with it. Use it only in an emergency situation.

Do you carry a knife of some type? If you have to use it, is it easily accessible? Personally, I always have a knife on me. Not really for personal defense, but more of a tool than anything. My everyday knife is one that I can open with one hand.

However, while on the water, you should have a good knife on you, somewhere easily accessible. There are knives made especially for "river rescue." Most of them have a serrated edge for better cutting, and a blunt tip to be used as a screwdriver, or a small pry bar. They also are held in their sheaths with integrated clips so that they do not fall out of their sheath. I believe there are companies that even make one with a bottle opener integrated into it. You don't necessarily have to have one of these types, but a good knife is good to have. We will go into knives a bit more later on in the book.

Next, is multipliers. You can get the full-size models that come in a sheath and fit on your belt, or smaller models you can buy that are compact enough to fit in your pack and not take up much room. These usually have both flathead and Phillips screwdrivers, pliers of course, maybe a file to sharpen a hook. I had to use them once to repair a wading staff that got stuck in the mud. The first thing I did thinking when the staff went down in the mud and wouldn't come out was trying to snatch it out. Holding the top section of the collapsible wading staff, I snatched it in an upward motion, and once the bungee cord inside stretched to its limit, the rest of the staff came slamming back together, and bent the connection point, and would not go back together correctly. Luckily, I had some multipliers to address the situation.

Folks, these few things I just went over are always handy to have. Hopefully, most of them you will never need, but it is good to have them just in case. The flashing light is good because it will draw attention. If you were to become immobile and you were able to call for help, hit the light and get the flashing going. Obviously the darker it is outside the better it's going to work but if someone is looking for you the flashing light will help. Most Fire, Rescue and EMS personnel love flashing lights. Now remember, the lights operate off of a battery, and of course it's not going to last forever, so to be on the safe side set a schedule to change the battery. You can put a reminder on your calendar on your phone or you can simply change it when you change the batteries in your smoke detector twice a year. To add to that, the whistle is a great attention getter. They can usually be heard from a good distance, and anyone with any Swiftwater Rescue training should recognize the sound of a whistle immediately, since they use them regularly in training. Also, a good knife. If you carry one on a regular basis, you know how much you use one. If you don't carry one, get one and you will be surprised how often you use it. Lastly, the multipliers. Another tool you will use more than you expected. You'll be surprised how much you will use them.

Chapter 8

Dam-Controlled Rivers

When I say dam controlled, I mean somewhere upstream, there is a dam that was built to form a lake for whatever reason. No, I am not *saying* "That damn, controlled river!"

Dam controlled is typically on a schedule made by the power company, or whomever may control it, that will open the flood gates to generate power and/or maintain a certain water level in the lake. The water below the dam is usually referred to as tailwaters. So, one thing to always remember while fishing in a dam-controlled river or "tailwater" is the term, "CFS"—not to be confused with CRS (Can't Remember Sh*t). CFS stands for Cubic Feet per Second, and it is defined by the National Weather Service as the flow rate or discharge equal to one cubic foot (of water, usually) per second. This rate is equivalent to approximately 7.48 gallons per second." Now a gallon of water weighs 8.34 pounds, but a cubic foot of water weighs 62.41 pounds!

Okay, with all those numbers floating around in your noggin, remember, CFS has a lot to do with rivers—or creeks in some cases—that have a dam upstream. Most of these dams are built to generate power. Water flows through turbines in the dam, which activate the generators to create power. So, they may have different times that are flowing water throughout the day as the demand for energy increases or decreases. Some of you may be thinking as you are reading this "Why are we talking about this?" Well, okay, say you are out on the river fishing at seven in the morning, and the stream flow is pretty good. A bit later in the day, you notice the flow seems to be getting a bit stronger for some reason. A few minutes ago, you heard what sounded like sirens blaring, but you paid no mind. The water seems to be moving faster and pushing harder. You also notice that the color of the water is changing a bit, and there's some debris coming downstream as well. All right, if you haven't figured it out yet, you are fishing on a dam-controlled river, and they have opened some of the floodgates to start making more power. The sirens you heard were not emergency apparatus. They are warnings to let anyone downstream of the dam, that floodgates are opening, so be prepared. Now you may be a good way away from the dam, but the water change will eventually reach you.

Good fly shops in the area should be able to give you a schedule of when the power company intends to generate power. Some power companies have it listed on their website. One thing you must remember, they may not always stick to the schedule. For some reason they may have to generate power for some unseen circumstance. This is why you need to be aware of your surroundings! You may not be close enough to hear the sounds of the sirens—or whatever type of warning system they may use—to inform the public that the dam is opening to flow more water. So, remember, if you feel the water is pushing harder, running faster, and maybe you notice the color of the water changing with a bit of debris, it's time to get out and take a break.

Two floodgates open to control the water level of the lake behind.

I have heard people say things like, "Well, if the water is running too fast for me to be comfortable, I just wedge my foot in between two rocks." Folks, this is what's known as a "foothold," and you do not want to do this. You may not be able to get your foot out. This also happens to be a very common way for people to break their ankle, and some even end up drowning. Some river bottoms may have a crack or crevice in the bottom that you could possibly step on, and your foot may become trapped in. This is something you need to be very careful of if you are trying to cross a river, especially if the water is moving fast.

While we are talking about dams, you must remember they come in all sizes and all types of construction. One type of dam I feel I should mention is a small dam called a "low-head dam." A low-head dam is usually built out of concrete, and of course, runs the width of the river or creek from bank to bank. Often, they're built to form a mill pond. They are usually short in height, so when the water crests, it will run over the top. There are no gates to open or shut—it is basically a wall built to hold back a certain amount of water.

One problem with this is, when the water is running high, it can form on the downriver side what is known as a "hydraulic." This also happens with natural waterfalls. What happens here is that since the water drops like a small waterfall from some elevation, the water creates a reverse formation of the water flow which in turn pulls the water back to the dam. This is a dangerous area to be nearby. Being caught in a hydraulic is very hard to escape. If you see a waterfall, look to the base of it and see if you notice some debris caught there. It usually spins in the opposite direction. The water is plunging down with such force it breaks the surface of and hits the bottom of the falls.

This is why low-head dams are referred to as "drowning machines." People have gotten trapped in these and were unable to reach the surface and drowned. There seems to be a growing movement across the country to remove these dams, since most of them have become obsolete.

Folks, you must remember, moving water is pretty much perpetual. Say it with me this time, water will not get tired, *you* will.

A dam at an old mill. Note the debris at the top of the dam.

Chapter 9

Fishing Close to Waterfalls

Almost like a moth to a flame, fishermen are drawn to waterfalls. It seems that some people become hypnotized and lose control when they get near one. "Ooh . . . waterfalls . . . pretty . . . must get closer."

Maybe it is more for the photographic opportunities than anything else. Every year people are injured or die around waterfalls. They are beautiful to look at but are very dangerous if you are not careful around them.

If you are at the top of the falls, it's pretty much self-explanatory. You slip, fall, and go over. Once you land at the bottom of the falls, gallons and gallons of water are going to beat you down, then at the bottom of the falls, there is the anomaly called a hydraulic.

Bald River Falls, near the Cherohala Skyway, Tellico Plains, Tennessee.

You should remember this from the previous chapter where we went over the low-head dams.

At the bottom of the falls, of course, you have all that water coming over and churning the water at the base. Due to this action, the water can become highly oxygenated and may attract some fish. However, you should remember to maintain a safe distance.

Remember water may not be the only thing that is going to come over those waterfalls. Debris in the form of tree limbs and whatever else that may be upstream, is eventually going to come crashing down on whatever is below. Next time you are at some waterfalls whether it be fishing or just viewing. Look around at the bottom of the falls and see if there is any debris. If there is now, think about if you were standing there when it came over!

If these waterfalls have easy access, then you will probably have to contend with crowds of people, and it will not be worth your time trying to fish there. If they are pretty secluded and you have to hike into them it may be a pretty good spot to fish. You must always remember though, the more difficult it is to get into, the more difficult it is to get out.

Waterfalls are generally very slippery due to a couple of different factors. One being the water itself. The continuing flow of water over the rocks can be almost like a polishing action. The water continuously carrying minerals and of course water, works almost like a very fine sandpaper continually smoothing the rock it travels over. Another contributor is Moss and algae, which thrive on the moisture from the cascades.

I thought I would add this into the book because accidents and drownings around waterfalls have seen a dramatic rise ever since the Covid pandemic.

Again, you must remember, lots of times these waterfalls can be in remote places. The harder they are to get to, the harder it's going to be to get you out, if you were to get hurt. Another reason to be aware of your surroundings.

Chapter 10

Wildlife Encounters

The word "wildlife" should be a dead giveaway, but for some reason, not everyone understands the term. In this term, I am also including insects and reptiles. Folks, there is an old saying that pretty much sums up an encounter with a lot of these creatures: *"You'd be better off trying to walk through Hell with gasoline drawers on than to tangle with one of them!"* I figured that may help get my point across.

Wild animals are not pets, nor are they friendly to humans. You should not approach them. If you get too close, they may see you as a threat, especially if they have young ones around. If they feel threatened, they may attack and guess whose fault that is. I'll give you a minute . . . okay, time's up, it's your fault! To them, this is a home invasion! You are the threat, and you must be eliminated, so they are going to do what they have to do. Folks, it does not matter how big and bad you think you are, or how fast you think you can run, my money is on the animal. Use some common sense, leave them alone and maintain a safe distance!

Another thing to remember, at certain times of the year it becomes mating season. Animals—especially the male animals—will become more aggressive and unpredictable depending on the season. To give you an example, a Bull Elk "in the rut." He's probably not going to look at you as the object of his desire, so don't worry about him humping your leg or anything like that. However, he may see you as a threat, and you must be dealt with. Now, you might have been the toughest guy on the block growing up, or you may be one of those MMA fighters, but this isn't going to mean a thing or impress this fellow. He's focused on eliminating the competition and he's eyeballing *you* as the competition.

When you go into a national park such as the Great Smoky Mountains, or Yellowstone, or anywhere there is wildlife, you must remember—this is not a petting zoo. These animals are not domesticated, meaning you cannot go up and pet them. They are *wild!*

If you have found a great fishing spot and are catching fish left and right, then all of a sudden, you see movement out of the corner of your eye. You turn to see it's a bear approaching what was *your* fishing hole.

Guess what? It's *his* fishing hole now. Maybe you think to yourself, *"Well I spent sixty dollars on this can of bear spray on my belt. I'll show him who this fishing hole belongs to."* Chances are you just wasted sixty dollars because that bear is sporting a fresh can of "whoop ass" and he's getting ready to open it up on you! There again, home invasion!

Something you have to remember about bear spray is that different manufacturers claim to have different effective ranges. Everything I have found varies from twenty feet to forty feet, and this is under ideal conditions. Wind is going to be a big factor in the spray pattern, this could easily decrease the effective range of the spray. You must consider the wind direction. One thing you definitely do not want to do is try to spray a bear if you are facing the wind. That can make a bad day worse.

Something else I must say about bears especially. If you see bear cubs, *then Mama ain't far away,* and she is going to be very protective of her babies. Do not go near the cubs! If you do approach them, the mama bear is going to see you as a threat and come after you. Avoid this situation altogether! Remember the thing about the gasoline drawers!

Another animal to watch out for is a cougar. I mean wild ones. Four-legged cougars, not the two-legged type. They are also known as mountain lions or panthers. These seem to be more prevalent in the Western US but occasionally do pop up in other parts of the country from time to time. They are beautiful animals, but they are *not* house cats. They possess the ability to sneak up on you before you realize they are there. These animals are excellent stealthy hunters and are very strong.

Remember, national parks and even state parks are animal sanctuaries. No hunting is allowed there. So, the animals can come and go as they please unless they become a nuisance, which is usually due to human interaction.

Let me say it again, you must be aware of your surroundings. Anywhere you go fishing, you should be aware of animals—and I mean *anywhere.* I say this is because animals are being pushed out due to overdevelopment. Animals are being pushed out of their habitats, or they are having to adapt to their new surroundings. This pretty much goes back to the "home invasion" thing.

Well, guess what? The big animals are not all you have to contend with. Another animal we need to talk about is snakes. Snakes being cold-blooded are usually more active in the warmer months.

You should really get familiar with what types of snakes are in the area's you fish, so you can learn to identify them. There are a couple of distinct ways to tell if a snake may be poisonous or not.

Usually, if the head has somewhat of a diamond shape to it, it is most likely a venomous snake. Another sign of venom is the pupil's narrow shape. Normally, if the head is not pronounced from the body, it's most likely non-venomous. Regardless, you don't want to be bitten by one of those either.

A black snake climbing down a tree. As you can see, the black snake is an excellent climber (non-venomous).

A rattlesnake lying in brush (venomous).

Now, being non-venomous does not mean that they will not bite! Yes, they *will* bite, and just because they aren't carrying venom doesn't mean you're out of danger. You see, I don't think snakes brush their teeth, and they probably don't use any type of mouthwash either. So, if you were to be bitten by a non-venomous snake, infection will be the biggest concern. If you get bitten by any kind of snake, seek medical expertise immediately. I know some of you aren't really wild about snakes so we will move on.

To . . . spiders! I know this probably isn't a real fun subject for some people, either, but they are out there. One of the worst things is walking into their webs. If you're fishing with a buddy, let them go first. Just make sure he's at least your height. If he's shorter than

you, well you're still likely going to get them in the face.

We do have a spider in my neck of the woods known as a "writing spider." They can get pretty big as far as spiders go, but they at least put some type of warning in their web. It's usually a white zigzag line in the very center of the web. They are not poisonous from what I understand, but they will scare the poo-poo out of you.

Two others that come to mind are spiders that are pretty bad news. One is the black widow. They are pretty easy to identify. Of course, they are black, they have a distinct shape, and the dead giveaway is the red hourglass shape on their abdomen.

Guess that's some type of warning.

And then we have the brown recluse. I'll bet you can't guess what color this little devil is . . . okay, it's brown. This little demon has a mark in the shape of a fiddle, or some say violin. No, I don't know why it has that. You'd think it would be a knife or a skull or something cool like that. Maybe it's something to do with the Grateful

A wolf spider on the side of an old building in the Great Smoky Mountains National Park

Dead or something. (Check out the Grateful Dead's album cover: Blues for Allah.)

Of course, spiders and insects tend to be out in the warmer months, so you don't have to worry about them too much all year long.

Fire ants. This is bad news as well. They are a problem because you may step on their ant hill without realizing it—well, at least for a little bit. Usually, when you do, they will hitch a ride on you and crawl up your waders in search of flesh to bite, and they can bite repeatedly. The problem with them is that they work off a "collective." So basically, when one detects a threat, the rest will know and it's time to go into attack mode.

I have noticed during flood situations, if ants get washed out of their mounds, they will group together and form a floating colony until they find something to climb onto to get out of the water. This can be debris floating downstream, rocks, or low-hanging tree limbs reaching into the water.

Now, let's talk about scorpions. According to my research, scorpions reside in the following states: Arizona, California, New Mexico, Nevada, and Texas. This really isn't surprising since most of these states have deserts. However, they also reside in Arkansas, Colorado, Illinois, Kansas, Louisiana, Nebraska, Oklahoma, Tennessee, and Utah.

Now I can tell you from personal experience—*yes,* they are in Tennessee! A few years ago, on a vacation to Eastern Tennessee, we had rented a cabin not too far from the Smoky Mountains National Park. The first night there, we spotted one. We figured, *"oh, well, that's unusual."*

A couple of days later, my wife was getting ready to put on her hiking boots, and low and behold, a scorpion fell out of the boot, and onto the floor. Okay, this is strange! So, upon check out, we go by the rental office to drop off the keys and we tell the kind lady there that there were scorpions in that house. She replied, "Yeah, we've had it exterminated a few times, but they just don't kill the scorpions." She just acted like it was not no big deal. So, I repeated, "Scorpions, not roaches!" She just nodded her head. Thinking that nobody would believe me I had killed one and put the remains in a zip lock bag. Later, while in the Smokeys, we ran into a park ranger, so I showed him the scorpion, and he replied, "Oh yeah, you must have been over near Strawberry Plains, they are all over that area." So, lesson learned. They exist in certain areas of the Southeast.

All right, earlier I said something about EpiPens and anaphylactic shock. If you have allergies to bee stings or any other types of insects bites you should have one of these handy at all times. If you are fishing with another person, then tell them, "Hey just in case, I am allergic to bee stings, I carry an EpiPen in my pack, so if I get stung this is where it's at and how to use it."

Other animals to watch out for during the day are nocturnal animals that are out during the daylight, such as foxes, skunks, and racoons. These creatures normally go on the move after the sun goes down. However, you may encounter them during daylight hours. If they see you first and run away, that's pretty normal, but if they stop and look at you, and/or approach you, it would be in your best interest to try and avoid them. There is a slight chance that they may have had some human interaction, maybe someone has been feeding them, but on the other hand, they may be infected with rabies. Rabies is transmitted through saliva, usually by a bite from one of these animals. If for some reason you are bitten by an animal, no matter if it breaks the skin or not, you should seek medical treatment immediately.

Skunks have a very unusual defense mechanism. They can spray a very unpleasant odor from their anal glands! Probably smelling worse than your buddy after they've had a couple of breakfast burritos the morning of your fishing trip. Also, it seems that skunks are found pretty much all over North America.

More bugs to watch out for are ticks. Another warm weather problem. There are a few different types of ticks, but I believe all of them do the same thing, they attach themselves to the flesh of their hosts—which can be you—and feed off blood. Another interesting fact is that ticks are known to be carriers of Rocky Mountain spotted fever and also Lyme disease.

Bees! Bees aren't typically too aggressive unless you accidentally run up on their nest or hive, then they are going to consider you a threat and swarm, and you could end up with multiple stings—which even if you are not allergic, you should seek medical help just to be on the safe side.

Yellow jackets. These devils will nest in the ground and probably come out of the depths of Hell. If you are not paying attention, you'll step on their nest, then there is Hell to pay. They come out in force, and unlike a honeybee that can only sting once, a yellow jacket can, and will, sting repeatedly. The problem is, if you piss one of them off, they will release a pheromone that alerts the rest of the hive then here comes the calvary. As an old friend of mine used to say, "You'd be better off trying to sandpaper a wildcat's ass, then mess with a yellow jackets' nest!" These reside all over the world but seem to be more abundant in the Southeastern US.

Hornets. These guys aren't really high on my popularity list either. Hornets generally build up in trees. Often, if you fish streams that have a canopy of trees over the water, you will probably run across a hornets' nest. If you do happen to see one, you may want to pass that area by, because if you accidentally hit it with your fly or even your fly rod, they are going to come out looking for you, and they will be pretty mad. Just in case you are not familiar, their nest kind of looks like the shape of an inverted teardrop. I don't believe they are as aggressive as yellow jackets, but I really don't care to feel their stings again either.

Of course, you cannot forget mosquitoes. Normally a bite from one of these isn't too bad. Usually just some localized redness and itching. However, there have been cases of West Nile virus that can be transmitted by mosquitoes. It is a good idea to have some type of insect repellant with you to use.

Another thing you may never see or have a problem with is leeches. A leech kind of resembles a snail but it's a lot flatter, and I believe they are actually considered to be part of the worm family. They don't seem to prefer cooler water or moving water, but this is still something to consider especially if you are "wet wading." Leeches are a parasite, and you may occasionally find one attached to a fish you caught. Leeches are not usually dangerous if one bites you, but the problem is in the removal process. If you grab it and try to snatch it off, this may cause it to regurgitate onto the bite and possibly cause an infection. Take something with a flat surface, such as a credit card or driver's license, and scrape it off to remove its mouth from your flesh. Then, some will treat the area of the bite with an antibiotic.

Now, I'm going to say it again. If you are susceptible to anaphylactic shock, get an EpiPen! Have it on you somewhere if you are out fishing. If you get stung, time is of the essence! I am telling you from my experience as an EMT, these save lives.

Another form of wildlife you may encounter in the water if you are in the Eastern or Central part of the United States is a very large salamander called a "Hellbender." If you happen to see one, it may scare the hell out of you, since they can reach just over two feet long and weigh up to five pounds, however, they are pretty much harmless. If you happen to see one, do not disturb it, but it would help if you reported the sighting to the local wildlife agency, since their numbers have been on the decline over the years. Spotting one of these in a stream is a good sign of water quality, since they require very clean water to survive. Now, I know the next question—*how did they get the name "Hellbender"?* Well, from my research, the most common explanation is because fishermen saw them and thought they were a creature bent on returning to Hell. I don't know how true that is, but it sounds good.

Folks, I cannot cover every single animal and insect all over the United States. If you are going to a different region of the country on a fishing trip, the best thing I can tell you is to use common sense.

If you see a nest or a wild animal, leave it alone and avoid it, if possible. You can do this, of course, by being aware of your surroundings . . . Do you get the feeling you have heard that somewhere before?

Stream Safety & Fly Fishing

A hornet's nest, high up in a tree.

The Elusive Red Balusha Spider

Now, maybe you have never heard of this spider. It's because it does not exist. This story came from a friend of mine I used to work with in the fire department. You see, we worked twenty-four-hour shifts, so once every month—in an effort to even out your time—you got a day or night off. This friend of mine, who shall be nameless, had a day off and came in that evening for duty. As with most professional firemen, he had a sideline job and it was painting houses. So, he had been off that day and came in for duty that evening. I was sitting outside the station when he pulled up in his car. He got out and approached me, rubbing his arm. When I noticed, I asked him, "What's wrong with your arm?"

So, he told me, "Well, I was up on a ladder painting some eaves, when I felt something on my arm, when I looked down and saw it was a spider! When I went to knock it off, I think it bit me." Then he said, "I hope it wasn't a Red Balusha!"

Of course, I questioned his last statement about the type of spider and he nervously repeated, "A Red Balusha." Again, I questioned him asking him if that was anything like a brown recluse. Well at this point, he knew he had screwed up again and he asked me, laughing nervously, "Well, you aren't going to say anything about this are you?"

And of course, I responded, "I will keep it quiet as long as I can." So, about forty-five minutes later, it accidentally slipped out. I don't know what I was thinking. But in front of the rest of the crew, I asked him how his arm was doing where the *Red Balusha* had bitten him, and they all turned around and immediately busted out with laughter. So, he had to explain himself and his statement, and we all had a good laugh about it.

Stream Safety & Fly Fishing

*A young Bull Elk hanging out on the stream.
Currently, the stream belongs to him!*

Chapter 11

Farm Animals, Pets, and Unattended Children

I want to say something before you read any further. The areas that will be mentioned such as the Blue Ridge Parkway, the Great Smoky Mountains, and any other National Park belong to all of us as United States citizens and are to be shared. However, a bit of courtesy should be shown to each other as well as the wildlife. But it never fails. I'll be fishing somewhere off the Blue Ridge Parkway or in the Great Smoky Mountains National Park, and I'll have the whole stream to myself before suddenly, I'll hear *it*. That dreaded sound! The shrill noise. If you don't know it yet, you will. It's the sound of a minivan, or possibly an SUV! They will pull up, resembling something from a circus. The doors fly open, and the kids begin pouring out, one after one! Finally, the dog comes out, and what does he do? He jumps in the water and comes over to me. I can't help but wonder what the poor animal is thinking after being cramped up with all those screaming children. Maybe the poor animal sees me as a brief moment of peace.

Once the parents exit the vehicle and see me standing in the water, they usually say two things: "Are you fishing?"

To which I want to reply, *"No, I am just standing in the water waving a fly rod around."*

Then the next question, *"Are you catching anything?"*

And being a purveyor of sarcasm, I always want to respond *with,* *"Well, not with your dog swimming around here now,"* but I bite my tongue, and try to say something less sarcastic.

Then the clowns—uh—kids run directly over to the water like it's a public pool or something. First, they must throw rocks in the water, then they jump in and splash, starting to scream. All the while, their parents are just oblivious to what their children are doing. Then, the "Death Knell" is when the parents pull out their folding chairs and flop down into them, pull out their phones and scroll through Facebook or whatever it is the careless parents do!

Okay, let's go on to something else—farm animals. Sometimes, you can go fishing somewhere close to a farm. Hopefully, the farmer is a good steward of the land and keeps his livestock out of the creek, but it's possible he may not. You may be fishing somewhere like this, and you must beware that the farmer may have a bull, and the bull could be a bit irritable. They may give some warning by stomping their feet a bit, bellowing at you, or snorting and blowing bull snot up in the air. You really don't want to tangle with one of these devils. If you happen to see one and he's out of his fence—*and you have never been employed as a rodeo clown*—you need to get out of Dodge! (That means vacating the area.)

The same can go for Billy goats. They are not in the same weight class as a bull, but they too may be on the irritable side and can still inflict injury. If you see one of these devils out, and if you notice them looking at you and putting their head down, they are getting ready to butt you. Here, again, you need to get out of Dodge! (Vacate the area,)

Lammas. Now there is one you don't have to worry about unless you get too close to them. Just pay attention if you do, because they are probably working up a big loogie to spit on you. This goes for alpacas too; they are spitters as well.

Horses are usually not too bad. Sometimes they can get kind of nosey and may want to come over and sniff you with those big horse nostrils—just keep your fingers crossed that they don't snort, leaving you covered in horse snot. I mean, next time you are around a horse, take a look at those nostrils. They can probably store a quart of snot in there!

Dogs. For whatever reason, some people let their dogs roam free. So, sometimes, when you're fishing, a dog may come up and visit you. Or he may wander around in the water a bit, screwing up your fishing. Some breeds of dogs, especially border collies, will seem to think your casting is a game of fetch. Honestly, they can't help it—it's in their nature. Every time you cast, they think you are throwing something *for them,* and they are supposed to go after it. Now, you have to be careful with this because you do not want to hook the dog. You can give up and go get in your vehicle, drive down the road, and the little fellows may follow you for a bit, but eventually, they'll go back to their house when it's time to eat. Dogs seem to be social animals. They like to get out and see what's going on.

Cats. Now *there* is a different animal. They can't be trusted. You never know what they are thinking. People who live nearby probably have a cat to keep the rodent population down. Cats will cover some territory too, but you still cannot trust them. They may wander up to you and want to rub on you, then they will turn around and pee on your high-dollar waders, or the cat may see them as a new scratching pad and try to *shred* your high-dollar waders! You cannot trust a cat. They can be a bit like the border collie, meaning they may see this casting thing as a game, and may want to go after your fishing line and/or fly.

Chapter 12

The Weather

Most of us watch the weather when we plan to go out fishing. If it's going to be hot or cold—if so, how hot or how cold? Let's say the forecast is for maybe a 10 percent chance of rain. Well, that's still a chance of rain. So, while you're on the way to the water, do you watch the skies? Do you take the time to look up and check while you're fishing? I know there are some streams that will fish better right after a light rain.

Consider this, where you are fishing, is it prone to flooding? What is the terrain like around where you are fishing? How about the color of the water? These are things you need to keep an eye on and watch out for.

Creeks and rivers in deep valleys, a gorge, or even in canyons with high walls are pretty much where all the softer stuff was washed away several thousand years ago but imagine how high the water was there at one time. And it could be again in certain conditions. A microburst thunderstorm can dump a lot of water in a short time and create a flash flood.

Ice melting from the previous winter can also raise the water levels. Check out a map of these different creeks and rivers and see how many tributary streams feed into them. If the map shows elevation, look and see how fast the terrain drops going downstream. This should give you an appreciation for the lay of the land.

To give you an example, in my neck of the woods here, in North Carolina, there is a creek called Wilson Creek. It originates at 5,946 feet above sea level at Grandfather Mountain and about 100 feet above the Blue Ridge Parkway. It flows downhill, of course, to the small communities of Edgemont, Mortimer, and Colletsville. It is a beautiful area down in the gorge, meaning it is surrounded by cliffs and mountains. By the time it reaches this area, it has become a river. This area has experienced some severe flooding over the years. So, with how the terrain is formed there, the water has nowhere else to go. It's not like flat land where the water can spread out over fields, it's all pretty much contained by the high walls of the gorge.

Grandfather Mountain is roughly thirty-three miles away from Colletsville. Now the elevation at Grandfather Mountain is 5,946 feet above sea level. The elevation of Colletsville is roughly 1,096 feet above sea level, so by the time Wilson Creek gets to the town of Colletsville, if you do the math, you can see that's a pretty significant drop—over thirty-three miles. Then you must factor in all the tributary creeks feeding in Wilson Creek along the way. So, if there were a big thunderstorm on a microburst up around Grandfather Mountain that dumps a lot of rain, it's got to go somewhere, and it's going to be downhill.

There are some interesting videos online about Wilson Creek and the towns around there. Mortimer was one that does not exist any longer because it was wiped out during a flood. There are some remains of old buildings there and a marker but that's about it.

Caruso and Canton, North Carolina, had more recent deadly floods. A tropical storm passing over the Blue Ridge Parkway dumped an immense amount of rain into the Pigeon River, which runs through the two towns and devastated the area. It was said that the river rose eight feet in a short amount of time.

This is why I say you need to be aware of the terrain you are fishing in as well as the weather around you. BE AWARE OF YOUR SURROUNDINGS.

There seem to be certain areas of the country where the weather can change rapidly, and sometimes, without warning. Having spent a lot of time on the Blue Ridge Parkway and in the Great Smoky Mountains, I have learned that this can happen in both of these areas. Temperatures can change quickly—it may be sunny one minute, then the clouds move in, bringing a tremendous downpour all of a sudden.

Always check and see if the areas you fish for are prone to floods and keep an eye on the weather.

You will want a good rain jacket handy. You may be warm enough, but if your clothes get soaked, the dampness is going to absorb your body heat and your core temperature is going to begin to fall, and you may run the risk of hypothermia. We talked about Hypothermia earlier in the book so you should be familiar with this term already.

If you're ready to make the purchase, there are several different manufacturers of rain gear with varying price options. Remember, though, like most things, you get what you pay for. I have a few different rain jackets I use, and they are pretty much "season specific." The one for spring and fall is fairly light, and easily packable, while the other is for colder weather, so it's a bit heavier.

One thing I would suggest is buying a good jacket and taking care of it. If you buy a cheap PVC jacket, you are going to burn up because it doesn't have any type of ventilation to it so you will begin to sweat which runs the risk of the hypothermia thing again. Most quality jackets are made of some type of fabric that has been treated to make it water-repellant, but you must remember, it may require additional treatments over time. This isn't an advertisement for this company, but I will say they make a pretty durable product. Anything made with Gore-Tex. This is something to look for in a jacket, because it's designed to be windproof, waterproof, and breathable. You can't ask for much more than that, but with this product, the price will go up. However, let me tell you from experience, if you buy something cheap and you get caught in a downpour, that cheap raincoat is only going to last so long! I can't tell you how many times I have seen people buy the most expensive fly rods with a luxurious reel and line, then buy cheap waders or rain jackets and end up getting wet.

Now talking about rain and rain jackets, this does not mean remain out there in the rain and you'll be okay. This is a situation where you have to use some common sense. How hard is it raining—is it supposed to get worse? What about thunder? You know what goes along with that . . .

Lightning! Folks, again, you must remember Mother Nature is *unpredictable!* I mean, think about it. A weatherman or a meteorologist is probably the only job you can have and be wrong

90 percent of the time and still be employed. But I digress. Lightning is unpredictable. You don't know where it's going to hit, or where it's going to move. Hopefully, far away from you!

But on to a bit of science—water is a conductor of electricity. A conductor is an object or material that allows the flow of a charge of electricity to travel in one or more directions. Now, with that in mind, you should remember, electricity is always looking for ground. So, if you are fishing or standing in the water, then you are standing in an electrical conductor, and also holding a nine-foot lightning rod in your hand. Guess what, you could be . . . a ground.

You can argue the conductivity of a fishing rod—graphite or fiberglass, or even bamboo. You can look it up online and see what it says about the conductivity of the different materials. While you are at it, see what it says about wood. Let me save you the trouble, it's a low conductor of electricity, but have you ever seen what happens to a tree when it is struck by lightning? Folks, electrical storms are no joke, get out of the water and to cover, as soon as possible.

So, let's move on to fog. You usually don't hear a lot about this, and a lot of people have probably never experienced this on a stream, but it is possible. Due to atmospheric conditions, fog can roll in unexpectedly and it can be rather unpredictable, meaning it can be light and somewhat transparent, or it can be very thick, where you can't see your hand in front of your face. And the problem this problem creates, of course, is visibility—or lack thereof. Imagine you are standing in the steam fishing, and a fog sneaks in on you—it's time to take a break and get out of the water. The problem here is how bad is the fog? Can you see far enough to get to the bank? What about what is in between you and the bank? Again, another argument for a wading staff.

Now to the other end of the spectrum from rain is the sun. A good sunscreen is good to keep handy, a long-sleeved shirt, and something to keep your head covered. This is a simple process—keep your bare skin covered. There are companies out there that make clothing just for this purpose, and it would be a good idea to invest in some. Your skin will thank you.

Now talking about the sun, you may be thinking about fishing somewhere like down at the Keys in Florida, Bonefishing in the Flats. Well, yes, that's true, but there are other places to consider you may not think about—like out West. The rivers in the West are usually a lot bigger and don't have a canopy of trees to cover them, so they are exposed directly to the sun, and the water tends to reflect the sunlight, which will intensify the UV rays by about 10 percent. Okay, now, you are probably thinking on a cloudy day I don't have to worry about UV rays . . . *Wrong!* If the sunlight can penetrate anywhere in the cloud cover, it's bringing the old UV rays with it. So, cover up. *How about snow?* Believe it or not, snow is a big reflector of UV rays. Fresh snow almost doubles the amount of UV rays.

While we are on the subject of the sun and UV rays, how about your eyes? Yes, the old eyeballs need protection as well. UV rays can wreak havoc on your eyes as well as your skin. Polarized glasses are very popular with fishermen because of the polarization process—it cuts the glare on the water, and in some situations, it even helps you to spot more fish. A good set of sunglasses will keep you from squinting, which may lead to headaches, and may also work as safety glasses to keep something from smacking you in the eye like a fishhook.

Now I consider a good set of glasses an investment. Just like the rain jacket, you'll get what you pay for. Go somewhere that will let you try them on and see how they fit—are they comfortable? If they are not comfortable, then you are not going to wear them, it's as simple as that. I prefer glasses that are called a wrap-around type. The reason for that is the wrap-around type doesn't allow light to sneak in the back side of the lenses. These really help when you are trying to tie on a fly. You don't have any glare coming in distorting your vision from either side.

Chapter 13

Personal Flotation Device

I do not wear a personal flotation device (PFD)—also known as a life jacket—when I am wading. Why? Well, it's my personal choice for one, but I also do not fish in water that's moving faster or deeper than I'm comfortable with. However, if I am going on a float trip, oh yeah, I will be wearing a PFD! These are some circumstances where I might wear a PFD:

- ➢ I am fishing out of a boat. This must mean that the water is fairly deep and it's probably a fairly wide body of water, therefore if I have to get to shore, I may have to do some swimming, and I could get tired before I get there, and the PFD will keep me afloat.
- ➢ Chances are, I may not know the person paddling the boat, so I don't know his experience level or expertise on handling a boat.
- ➢ If I were to fall out of the boat, is the person paddling the

boat going to know what to do? Is he going to remain calm and be able to help me or is he going to freak out and panic and be more of a problem than a help?

> I may be in the water for a while, so I don't need to waste any energy. I need to remain calm and figure out if the person in the boat is going to be of any help, or do I just float to the shore, and get out on my own. Now, something I have never really understood. Having the PFDs stored somewhere on the boat. Well, that's fine as long as everything goes well, but if you were to fall out of the boat or say the boat hit some rough water and flipped, you may be disoriented temporarily. If this were to happen because of some rapids in the water, the situation may be worse. Believe me, falling out of a boat into some rapids, you are at the mercy of the water, but a PFD will increase your chances of survival tremendously.

Now, if you fall into cold water, it gets worse. Falling into cold or frigid water can cause you to and possibly hyperventilate. Due to the sudden shock to your system, it could also make your heart rate and blood pressure spike.

Folks, this is my personal opinion, I believe all guides in all states must be required to take a class, then pass a test to be a guide and required to be insured.

With all of that being said, you may think this does not apply to you. You may be a pretty good swimmer—even a real Mark Spitz (1972 Summer Olympics). But think about how often you go swimming in several layers of clothes and wearing wading boots. All this extra stuff you have on is going to weigh you down, slow you down, and tire you out. But consider this . . . with all of the stuff you have weighing you down in the water, then you have the current carrying you away. It's not a good situation to be in. It's not like swimming in a pool wearing a set of "plum smugglers" (Speedos).

Something you might consider is investing in your own PFD if you plan on doing a lot of float trips. This way you can get one that fits you well, and that you will be comfortable in it. I would say go somewhere that has a lot of PFDs in stock so you can try it on and make good movement while you are fishing. You'll know for sure how the vest has been stored and treated. Be sure to look inside the PFD and make sure it is Coast Guard Approved.

There are a lot of different types of PFDs on the market now, so you'll have different styles to choose from. Some of the more comfortable types are vests. They tend to give you a bit more freedom and are less cumbersome. There are even manufacturers out there that have integrated a fly vest into a PFD. Additionally, there are also inflatable vests on the market now that give you more freedom of movement. These come in a couple of different versions, one being automatic, and the other manual. The automatic version inflates—*you guessed it, automatically*—when you fall in the water. However, if for some reason it does not inflate automatically, it has a manual pull tab to activate it. The manual model simply has the pull tab you must pull to activate it. These types of vests will require a bit more maintenance since they have a CO_2 cartridge used for inflation. So, if you use it once, then you will have to replace the cartridge. The cartridge may have an expiration date as well, so you will have to keep track of that to make sure it's still in date. These types of vests are fine, but I believe if you are in moving water, a regular vest is a better choice because you don't have to worry about whether the vest is going to inflate or not. Basically, there are fewer moving parts, so to speak.

You must remember, this is not a fashion show, folks. So, you shouldn't buy a PFD because it looks cool. You should get one that is going to support your weight and is going to be comfortable. You may have to spend a bit more money to get this, but in the long run it will be worth the investment. For visibility purposes, another thing to consider is the color of the vest. You will want something bright in a worst-case scenario, so you can easily be found. Believe me, during a "search operation" a brighter color is a lot easier to spot than a dark color.

Chapter 14

Dress for the Weather

Common sense plays a big part in this next bit we are going to go over. The weather can be pretty unpredictable in some of these areas we fish, so you need to keep that in mind when you are planning your attire for the outing.

In colder weather, you should dress in layers. Your first layer, such as thermal underwear, should be a good product that has the ability to wick moisture away from your skin. You want to stay away from cotton products. Remember the term "Killer Cotton"? Cotton is a fine material, but not in this situation because cotton tends to hold moisture, so any perspiration will be absorbed by the cotton and not wicked away.

Your next layer of clothing should be for warmth as well, but you should wear something comfortable. The reason I say this is because if you aren't comfortable, you aren't going to be able to concentrate on fishing, or other things you need to be paying attention to, and little things like this can really ruin a good fishing trip.

Remember, you need to focus on your core temperature where most of your vital organs are, and they like to maintain a regular temperature. This is one reason your hands and feet will start to get cold—because your body is trying to maintain temperature around your vital organs. Which leads me to the next article of clothing— a pair of quality socks. I can't say this enough because if you are standing in forty-degree water for extended amounts of time, a durable pair of socks are important to have. Over the calf socks are really a big help in times like this. They will add an extra layer of insulation to your lower extremities. Now, if you plan on wearing over-the-calf socks and regular underwear, this leaves a gap between your knees and your thighs. Well, let me tell you, I tried this once, thinking I would be warm enough . . . *Nope!* My calves were warm, but my thighs froze. So, lesson learned! I always wear long underwear with over-the-calf socks.

Something else to help keep your hands and feet warm are a couple of different items. You may remember the old hand warmers you filled with lighter fluid, then you lit the burner and put the top back on, and it stayed warm for several hours? Well, actually, they are still being made, but with new technology, they are rechargeable hand warmers now. You just plug them into a USB port and let them charge up, then they are ready to go. Some claim to last over ten hours. "Hot Hands" is another item that seems to work pretty well and requires no batteries, but because of that they are only a one-time use. These are air-activated. Once you open up the package, they come in and after a minute or so they have warmed up.

For your upper half, you also should have a good toboggan or some type of insulated hat to keep your head and ears warm. For years, it was said you lose most of your body heat through your head. In my research, I found this idea comes from a study that the US Army did back in the '70s, but as of late, it seems to be disputed by today's medical society. My mom was never in the Army, but she always made sure I had something on my head in cold weather, and yes, I still choose to cover my noggin), especially since I don't have as much hair up there anymore. Doctors and scientists can say what they want, but I can surely tell a difference in temperature, or a breeze on my head these days.

We have already talked a bit about clothing for warmer weather earlier in the book. Such as clothing that will help block the sun—long-sleeved shirts, and such. With today's technology manufacturers are able to build material that will block out harmful ultraviolet rays and you won't feel like you are wearing a sauna suit that was popular back in the '70s and '80s.

Again, we're going to talk about your head. Don't get complex! Keep it covered while you are out there in the sun—especially if you are like me and don't have as much hair up there as you used to!

Chapter 15

Fishing with a Buddy

Fishing with a buddy can have advantages and disadvantages. Some of the disadvantages are waiting for them to get ready to leave and get out on the water. Some may be a real diva that has to have their hair just right before they leave or wear the latest gear—you know, the ones with all the labels everywhere. Maybe they worry about getting their new waders dirty while getting in or out of the water. You also have the type that gets pretty gassy after stopping to get a breakfast burrito on the way to the creek then like to "fluff one," and lock the windows as you are going down the road. I could go on and on about the things we do to antagonize one another, but there are a lot of advantages to fishing with a buddy.

It is a good idea to fish with someone else. You'll always have help in case something happens. If you fish with someone on a regular basis, the two of you should know each other pretty well. I mean, if one of you takes a certain medication or has an ailment of some kind so you can look out for each other.

For instance, say your buddy is diabetic. The morning of your big fishing trip, you stopped at the Hook, Line and Sinker restaurant on the way to the river and had breakfast. He's the one that had the breakfast burrito! Anyway, that was about seven in the morning. After you guys have been on the water for a few hours, your buddy is acting a little differently. This is where you say, "Hey, you want to stop and grab some lunch?" Since it's been a few hours since he ate, his sugar may be getting a little out of whack, so he needs to eat something to get straightened out.

Another scenario. Your buddy does not use a wading staff because they think it makes them look old. So, he takes a bad step onto a moss-covered rock, his foot slips, and he goes down, injuring his knee. They try to get up but can't put weight on it because it hurts too bad. But luckily, he has a buddy—this would be you!

You have to help him get out of the water, back to the vehicle, and possibly to a hospital, where you will have to help them get inside.

This is another situation where it pays to be aware of your surroundings. If there is someone else fishing nearby, you may be able to get their attention to give you some help. However, there's also the chance no one is around.

Watch out for each other and anybody else around that may be fishing nearby! People can disappear quickly. Say your buddy who had the breakfast burrito had to run off because it was knocking at the door, and he had to go up to the woods. Seriously though, anything *could happen,* and you may not know. We get complacent out there and have the "never happens to me" attitude *until* it happens to you.

In situations like this, these are the times to know each other's medical issues, if either of you have any. If either of you are allergic to insect bites or stings and you have an EpiPen, tell your buddy where you have it and how to use it. Same goes for a heart patient. If you carry a prescription bottle of Nitroglycerin, tell your buddy where it's at, just in case.

In lieu of these situations, if you do experience a situation where you have to administer a dosage of any type of medication, do not continue fishing. Seek medical help immediately! Just because you feel better right now, does not mean everything is okay.

Look at it this way, you'll have your buddy around a few more years and you can always remind them how you had to single-handedly carry them back to the truck, which was uphill of course, at least two miles, *and* you had to fight off two wolves, a cougar, and a cocaine bear before you got back to the truck. Hey, it's your story—embellish it all you want. It'll get better every time you tell it!

Folks, having fishing buddies is really an important thing to have. None of us are going to live forever. Get out with your buddy and go fishing and enjoy each other's company before it's too late.

Chapter 16

Hydration

It is always good to have some water in hand. If you don't have a place to keep a bottle in your pack, then keep it in your vehicle and take a break every so often to go back and drink some. Try and make it a habit to bring some water with you every time you plan to go out fishing. Buy yourself an insulated bottle. That way you won't have another plastic bottle to recycle. Or get yourself a quality cooler and throw some ice in with some bottled water. Some of the packs that are being manufactured now actually have a place to carry a water bottle, which is convenient.

I know what some of you are thinking, why not drink some water out of the river?

Well, you really don't want to do that. There is so much stuff that could be in the water these days. One really bad thing that could be in the water is something known as giardia. This comes from feces that may find their way into the water, usually from an animal, or even a human that has already been infected with giardia. The results from this can be extreme diarrhea, among other things. I know you've seen the old cowboy movies where the cowboy rides his horse up to the creek and they both drink water. Well, that's Hollywood—and you can't believe everything you see on the silver screen.

Folks, you might be fishing the most pristine river in the middle of nowhere that has been protected for years from development and anything else. Not a building for as far as you can see. The water may be as clear as a good jar of moonshine (Not like I would know; I saw it on a television show!) Anyway, you would still be taking a risk drinking that water. Somewhere—probably upstream—there is probably a big deer using the stream for a bathroom.

Think about this next time you're fishing somewhere, and you will notice a cow pasture nearby. Cows pretty much eat and poop as they graze. All that poop sits there until a really good rain washes away—and where does it go? Downhill. And what is at the bottom of the hill? The water you are fishing in. Do you still want to drink it now?

If you must drink water from the creek or river, get yourself a good filtration system, preferably one that filters out bacteria and other contaminants. These filtration systems can get a bit pricey, but if you are going on a trip where you hike to spend the night, a good filtration system is worth it. You don't want to get sick while you are back there in the woods.

Another thing that can play a part in hydration is altitude—meaning a gain in altitude. This is something a lot of people don't ever think about or know about. The higher you go in altitude, the more hydration your body loses. This is a bad deal and something you should be aware of and keep this in mind. So, if you're planning a fishing trip somewhere in the Rocky Mountain range, this is something you should remember. This may sound a little extreme, but it can happen. There is a lot of good information online about this particular subject, and I would suggest if you happened to have a lung condition or something you should consult a professional on this before you go.

Some of the signs of dehydration are dry mouth, fatigue, feeling light-headed, less frequent urination, dark-colored urine, and confusion.

Now, I'm probably going to step on a few toes again. Drinking alcohol is not hydration. Actually, it is just the opposite, believe it or not. Now if you are still reading and have not closed the book by now and thrown it against the wall and cursed at me, then keep reading.

Alcohol is what is known as a diuretic. A diuretic is roughly defined as increased passing of urine. You pee a lot. Therefore, you are not retaining the water you need because you are releasing it every time you urinate. The higher the alcohol content, the greater the chance of dehydration. Folks, I'm not saying you can't drink a couple of cold beers while you are out there, but you might want to exercise some self-control. Throw a few bottled waters in the cooler with the cold beers.

Chapter 17

Things to Watch Out for While on the Stream

Streams, creeks, and rivers are pretty much like highway systems. Just like on the road, goods and other items are transported from place to place. Streams transport sediment, debris, and whatever else is downstream from point to point. However, a lot of this stuff is simply going along for the ride. It's going along at the mercy of the current, it does not care what is in the way—whether it be a bridge, a big rock, or if it may happen to be you. It's a natural process, a big storm comes and washes everything out to the low-lying areas, which is usually where the streams are. Then the streams carry it away. When a big storm hits and washes out a creek or river, carrying a lot of stuff away it exposes new soil and stone. However, during this process, a lot of debris can be created and become trapped sometimes impeding the flow of the stream.

Some of the things that help create these obstacles are usually man-made but then again some are of a natural process as well.

Stream Safety & Fly Fishing

When a creek bank or riverbank gets washed out, it does a few different things. It can undercut a tree, and the tree may fall across the creek. It then becomes a "strainer," meaning it traps other debris coming downstream. But sooner or later, the strainer is going to fail due to the constant force of the current continually pushing against it or could simply begin to rot away and start breaking up, sending debris downstream. Remember what I said earlier about fishing upstream? If you see debris like this coming downstream, the best thing to do is leave it alone and let it go. Why? Well, for one, it may be heavier than you think, and you may end up injuring yourself trying to divert it or pull it out. It could be a fence post from an old farm or something with barbed wire attached to it. You may not notice it, until the barb wire catches your waders and rips a hole in them, or worse, catches a body part and cuts into your flesh. There could be an animal hitching a ride on it who's not really friendly. It may sting or bite. These things can be traveling faster than you think they are, and again, you are standing on an uneven surface. This can be a recipe for disaster. If you know there is someone fishing downstream you should make them aware of the debris headed their way. A good whistle would help in this situation!

A downed tree from a washed-out bank creating a "strainer."

Big rocks are notorious for catching debris and due to their unusual shape, they may hold debris for a while, but they also may work like a chute by diverting the debris in a different direction, making things a bit unpredictable.

Typical "low water" bridge.

Bridges are also catching debris around their pylons. However, some of the worst bridges for this are the low-water bridge. These bridges are just what they call them. They usually have only a couple of feet between the bottom of the bridge and the surface of the water. I would say these bridges are usually in places that are very rural and may not be on a main thoroughfare—typically one lane. Anyway, with them being so close to the water's surface, during a storm or flood, they will probably be submerged until the water recedes, but in the process of the high and fast water, they will become strainers.

Unstable banks are another thing to watch out for. This is something that can happen after a big storm, or snow melts like in the western states. This is due to the rapid water rise. Basically, what happens is all this water is suddenly introduced into the system and follows the path of least resistance, eroding banks out, as it makes its way to lower ground. The problem is, you  really can't see that the bank you may be standing on has been undercut, and therefore, has no support under it. Then it collapses and you are going in the water, unexpectedly! This is another situation for a good wading staff. As you walk closer to the bank, use the staff as a probe, jabbing it onto the ground. If it's unstable, it will penetrate the ground, or the ground may simply crumble and fall into the water. If you notice the other side of the stream has undercut banks, there is a good chance the bank on your side may be undercut as well. Just be careful.

In my experience, some of the best fishing is after a light rain, not a "Frog Strangler" (heavy rain), but this does not mean you should be unaware of debris heading downstream.

Debris can be lodged somewhere for a long time, then finally from the constant beating of the current, or some other reason, it can break loose and head downstream. It may be one piece of debris, or it could be one piece that was *holding back* a bunch of debris. Then, all of a sudden, it's going for a ride, possibly heading in your direction. This type of thing is really unpredictable, this is why you should always be on the lookout to avoid this situation.

Chapter 18

When Nature Calls

Okay, folks, in the process of writing this book I have tried to think of everything I have experienced in my time and everything I could think of.

I really didn't think this particular subject should be left out. It's a natural fact, sooner or later, we are all going to have to use the bathroom. Now for us guys, going and peeing isn't a real problem, but for the ladies in the crowd, it's a bit more involved.

However, for both genders—when you have a "Code Brown coming down"—well, that is a bit more involved. In lieu of this situation—as I mentioned earlier—something you should try to remember is where fire stations may be just in case, try to remember where public restrooms are located—just in case. You may be fishing in a national forest, national park, and in some state parks, there are usually some facilities somewhere nearby—just pay attention and try to remember where they are.

Pit latrines or pit toilets are just a fancy word for an outhouse. Okay, for those of you who are of the younger generation, an outhouse is what people had for a bathroom before there was indoor plumbing. Basically, there was a deep hole dug into the ground, and a small shack built over it. Then inside it had almost a boxed, bench seat built in the back of it with a large hole or two cut out for seats. Yes, folks, this is where you went to do your business. It was usually built somewhere downwind of the house and away from water sources such as a creek. Today you will see modern versions of these in very remote places such as state parks, national parks, and national forests. One thing I remember my grandparents telling me, before sitting down you had to beat on the wood around the seat to make sure there were not any black widow spiders anywhere around the underside of the seat. This may have been an old wives' tale or a joke or something, but just in case!

Another "just in case" situation, you can keep a roll of toilet paper, baby wipes, or some type of wet wipes strategically placed somewhere in your vehicle. So, if you can't find a bathroom or can't make it to one, you've got something to "finish the paperwork" if you know what I mean.

Now if you do some investigative research on your own, you'll find different items to accommodate you better for this situation. There are companies out there that offer toilet seats that fit into the receiver hitch on your truck, but if you want some privacy while you are doing your business, you'll have to improvise. I have also heard of some people carrying a bucket just for this purpose. There are all types of camp toilets. If you do an online search, you will find you have all types of options. The problem is the lack of privacy. This is why I look for public restrooms on the way to where I'll be fishing and try to remember just in case.

While we are on this subject, a lot of wader manufacturers are offering waders now with a zip front. I invested in a set, and I love them. It makes it a whole lot easier, especially for these situations. I tested the zipper by going about waist-deep in water just to see if they would leak and they held up. The zipper front also can work as a thermostat. So, if you begin to get too warm, you can open the zipper a bit to let out some body heat—or a bit of flatulence if your buddy is nearby.

Folks, if you go on vacation and plan to do some fishing, you are probably going to try some different foods somewhere and they may not sit well with your system, meaning they may have some adverse effects due to some different seasoning or whatever. It may not agree with you, let's say. That's why it's always good to have something like antacid on-hand to settle your gut, so it doesn't ruin your underwear—I mean, your trip!

A friend of mine and I were coming back from a fishing trip one day, and we were driving two different vehicles. We were coming up on the turn to get on the interstate, when all of a sudden, he crossed over about three lanes and pulled into a convenience store. I finally got turned around and pulled into the convenience store parking lot, not understanding what was wrong. I saw him coming out the door, so I asked him, "What happened?" He told me *the pain* hit, and he had to go! He said he got out of the truck and was walking across the parking lot and walked in the door, and before he could say anything to the man working there, the man pointed and exclaimed, "The bathroom is back there!" and pointed. The next thing he said was, "I recognize the walk!"

Always remember the old saying, "Never pass a urinal, and don't trust a fart!"

Chapter 19

Hiking into the Backwoods, to a Stream

Notice all the exposed roots creating "trip hazards."

Let's say you get the big idea of doing some Blue Line fishing. The term "Blue Line" typically means fishing small remote streams for native trout.

This may even be something that will take you some time to get in somewhere—possibly even pitching a tent and spending a night or two at the location. If you plan on going alone, which I don't recommend, you should let somebody know where you are going and when you plan to be back. If there is a ranger station in the area, you may be required to get a backcountry permit. These are usually required in national parks and national forests. One of the reasons for this is so they can keep up with you and be aware there is someone in the forest. That way, you don't have to worry about the government thinking you are going to run up on a top-secret site or something. It's mainly because if you don't come out of the woods at a designated time, they may have to come in looking for you in case you got lost or hurt, and you can't get out under your own power.

If you are going to plan on doing this, you need to watch an old Clint Eastwood movie called *Dirty Harry*. The reason I say this is because he had a saying in this movie: "A man's got to know his limitations," and you should too. Hiking and carrying all your supplies on your back—be it for the day, or a couple of days—takes some time to prepare. If you are not in shape for an endeavor like this, then you should start exercising and get your body in shape. Too many people start a hike ill-prepared, find out it's not as easy as they had anticipated, and end up in trouble. Do you want your friends to see you on the news again in another situation that they are going to tease you about forever?

Trips like this will also require equipment. Sure, you can go into the big box stores and talk to someone who works there that may not have any idea of what they are talking about, or you can shoot in the dark and go online and order something. My suggestion is to find a small shop, locally—somewhere that specializes in this type of equipment. Employees that can recommend something to you because they have actually used something similar or at least have some knowledge of it. Now if you have a decent fly shop you deal with, then they also should be able to help you with a good selection for flies and other equipment better suited for Hiking in.

Again, you must be aware of your surroundings. Pay attention to the landmarks going in because you should be seeing the same ones on the way out. Also, you need to be watching for "trip hazards" so you don't fall and bust your *"bootius* maximus."

Folks, I will tell you from personal experience in these situations, a good pair of hiking boots and durable socks will make a tremendous difference. If you get a blister on your foot on the hike out, it's going to make a long walk feel even longer.

There are some fly-fishing-related companies that are making backpacks for this type of fishing. You should check with your local fly shop to see if they carry any of these. I highly recommend trying one on before you buy it to make sure it fits your frame.

Also, as we talked about in an earlier chapter, GPS units and personal location beacon, and Satellite Emergency Notification Devices can be a real help in these situations. If you are going to have these devices, then you should be aware of all their features and how to use them. Don't wait until the night before you go to try to learn to use them. It should be second nature to you. Again, if you are considering one, you must remember they may require a subscription. If you do like to hike to fishing spots, I believe it would be a good investment on your part.

Another thing you must remember—the trails you are using are probably being used by the locals as well. When I say the locals, I mean wildlife, of course. So, as you are moving along watching for trip hazards and such, you also should look for wildlife tracks.

You can study charts and learn how to identify tracks of what may have made that track, but I stick to the simple philosophy—big print, big animal. These paths or trails can tell you a lot. If the grass and brush are pretty worn down, then the terrain is being used pretty regularly. Aside from tracks, a couple of things to look for is scat—or poo-poo. If you see how dry or moist it may be, it will give you an idea of how long ago something has passed through there. Nevertheless, this is a definite sign wildlife uses this as well.

Another indicator is hair. Often, animals such as deer or bears passing through, may catch some hair on briars, or other types of brush, leaving a sign they are in the area. This is a time when you should be using all of your senses, continually watching for the signs we've gone over. If you're paying attention, you may hear animals making noises as they go about their way, or even some type of noise to alert that you are approaching their territory. Of course, there is always smell, but by the time you smell something, you may have already stepped in it.

I always use my wading staff as a hiking stick when walking trails to fish. It helps me with maintaining my balance on the trail, of course, but it also comes in handy when I run up on a spider web. Spiders are notorious for building their webs across a path or trail. If you aren't paying attention, you will walk right into it, and you'll end up wearing it! It's likely you will also end up with a hitchhiker on you somewhere. Got chill bumps yet?

Moving on, we have already talked about wildlife encounters in a previous chapter. Again, let me reiterate! These are wild animals. You have no idea how they are going to react to your presence. *Do not approach them!*

A few items I suggest you throw in your pack before you go:

➢ Paracord. This stuff almost rates up there with duct tape. You can use Duct tape for all types of things.

➢ A small roll of duct tape, just in case.

- A signal mirror. These require only sunlight, no batteries. These can be a very powerful way to get attention if you require help.
- A small first aid kit, or a small collection of medical supplies.
- A couple of protein bars among other foods, and a small water filter.
- Waterproof matches and a Ferro rod also.
- Personal Locating Device.
- Wet wipes, baby wipes, or toilet paper for when nature calls. Believe me, you don't want to accidentally use poison ivy leaves—that can lead to a bad situation. (Another disclaimer, this never happened to me).
- A couple of chem lights. The nice thing about these is they don't require batteries.
- Moleskin is good to have in case you get a blister on your foot.
- An emergency blanket.
- A compass and a map. However, before you take off, you need to learn how to use a compass, learn how to read a map, and be proficient in doing so. You can check with your local camping store and see if they have anyone there proficient in this or you may have to resort to the internet.

With all of this being said, you should try to keep your pack thirty to forty pounds. You may need to do some dry runs to get ready and make sure you are up to it. You might be able to *reach* your destination, but you want to be able to make it *out* as well. You don't want your buddy to have to carry your gear—you know that you would never hear the end of that.

Okay, remember reading about fishing with a buddy? Well, this is the prime example of why you *should* fish with a buddy. Folks, I cannot stress enough for you to not do this alone! If you want to hike somewhere and fish, find yourself a buddy who will go with you. Remember, somebody has got to live to tell the story!

Chapter 20

Have a Good Knife

As I've mentioned already, I carry a knife on me regularly. A fellow I used to work for had a saying when someone asked him if he had a knife, he always responded with, "I got my pants on, don't I?" That was basically his way of saying yes. I don't walk out the door without my knife, and I damn sure don't walk into the woods without it either.

A good knife is a tool. If you don't have one or carry one, you will be surprised how much you can use it. If you go online and research knives, you will see there is a plethora of choices. But if you think you need a big Rambo knife, or a big Bowie knife—this is kind of overkill. There are different styles and types of knives out there, and with a little research, you can become well-versed. The everyday knife I carry is a folding knife, which we will talk about later in this chapter, but when I'm going into the backwoods, I prefer to carry a Camp knife. The blade is probably around four inches long and has a very thick spine that runs the length of the handle. Another good blade style I suggest is a Kephart-style blade. This too is a good general-purpose style blade for the backwoods. If you go online and type in Horace Kephart, you will find the interesting history behind this style of blade.

As I said before, if I am going on a backwoods stream where I have to hike into the stream, I prefer to have a straight-blade knife in a sheath. One reason is because, unlike a folding knife, it has no moving parts, so there is really nothing to accidentally malfunction. However, I normally have my everyday knife on me as well, which is a folding knife.

A quality knife should be easy to use and comfortable in your hand. If not, then you are probably not going to want to use it as much and be disappointed. It should also be comfortable to wear or carry. A knife that is too big is going to be heavy and more than likely uncomfortable to carry.

Blade steel is very important as well. Some forms of steel will hold an edge or stay sharp longer than other types of steel. Some are prone to rust, so will require a bit more maintenance. So, this is also something to consider.

Have you ever heard the expression: "Like a Swiss Army knife"? Well, if you don't know, a Swiss Army knife is a real thing and has been around a long time. These knives come in all types of configurations, with options like magnifying glass, scissors, corkscrews, bottle openers, saws, and so much more. A very interesting knife, very handy, but remember the more attachments you have to a knife, the heavier it will be.

After you get a good idea of what type of knife you want to purchase, I would suggest going somewhere where you can look at the knife in person and handle it to make sure it's what you want. It seems when the internet came along, a lot of knife shops were on the decline. However, there are few good places to find one such as a gun and knife show. The vendors will have them on display, and you will be able to handle them to see how they feel and how comfortable they are in your hand.

As I've mentioned, my "everyday knife" is a folding knife. It has a pocket clip on it, so it stays in place all the time. That way, when I need it, I don't have to plunder through my pocket trying to find it. Also, it has the ability to open with one hand, which makes it very handy. However, when I go fishing or if I'm going into the backwoods, I prefer a straight knife which has a sheath to store it in. The reason for this is because it basically has no moving parts.

During my Swiftwater Rescue training I learned about a particular type of knife called a "River knife." This is, of course, a specialized knife designed for rescue operations. It has a short stout blade with a blunt tip. Usually, only these knives will have either a partially serrated edge or possibly a fully serrated edge for cutting rope and such. The sheath is usually a retaining type that will hold the knife in place, so it doesn't fall out while it's not in use. The sheath is also designed to be inverted so it can be easily mounted to a lash tab on a PFD.

When purchasing a knife, remember, you get what you pay for. The material used to make the knife will have a reflection on the price of it.

Fair warning, if you do your research on knives, such as blade materials, handle materials, and grinds and such, you are going to go down the proverbial "rabbit hole," so be careful. It can be an information overload!

Lastly, I will say, don't get attached to your knife. If you have one that has been a family heirloom, you may want to leave it at home because there is a chance you may lose it or damage it.

Chapter 21

Carrying a Firearm While Fishing

Okay, folks, I made jokes and maybe told a couple of funny stories in the process of this book, but right now it is time to be serious. Maybe just this chapter anyway. This area can be a sensitive subject, so before I go on, I am saying right now—this is not a political statement. I am not saying you should or shouldn't carry a firearm. This is a personal choice. I'm just saying if you choose to legally own and carry a firearm, you are taking on a tremendous responsibility. You need to understand that. Also, if you choose to do this, you need to get professional training in how to handle it and should be proficient at it. You should not only learn how to shoot it, but you should learn how to maintain it and how to properly clean it. As a firefighter and an EMT, I did respond to a few accidental shootings when someone was trying to clean up a gun. Remember, you should always treat a gun like it is loaded.

Now folks, there is a lot of common sense that comes into play here. If you are out in the woods and you see a snake, don't shoot it just because you *have* a gun. Leave it alone and let it go on its way. This also goes for the rest of the wildlife out there.

If you do not currently own a weapon but are planning on buying one, my advice to you is to go to a gun range that has guns to rent. If you are interested in a particular gun, you can rent it first and shoot it to see if you may be comfortable with it or not. Believe it or not, some handguns will be more comfortable than others. If you ever have to use it in this case, you want to be comfortable with it. By doing this, you will know you are comfortable with how the gun feels, in addition to the recoil. It is an excellent way to try before you buy. Some gun ranges even offer classes on gun safety, which I do recommend. Believe me, I have bought guns before without shooting them, and then after I shot it a few times, I found out they just were not comfortable for me to shoot.

Semi-Auto or Revolver. It seems over the past twenty years or so that semi-autos have been more in favor of the two. Probably because of their capability to have a greater ammo capacity. On the other hand, revolvers are a bit more simplistic than the semi-autos and not as finicky when it comes to different loads of ammo. This too is a personal preference, and this is why I say go to a range where you can't rent one and see what your preference may be. Deciding to purchase a handgun can be quite expensive, and in a lot of places, the sales are final, so you want to make sure you are going to be satisfied with your purchase.

Earlier, when I said to be proficient with a gun, I meant having very good aim. This also falls under the responsibility of training with it. If you have to use it, then shot placement is paramount. For example, if a large animal sees you as a threat, charges you, and you must make the decision to draw your weapon and stop the threat, shot placement is going to make the difference. You may be carrying a 9mm with fifteen rounds in it, but if you can't hit the broadside of a barn with it, you are wasting your time. Also, just because you have fifteen rounds, doesn't mean you should depend on all of them. If you do not hit your target, that bullet is going to continue until it impacts something else. I know these can be harsh words, but it's the simple truth. Personally, if you do decide to carry a firearm, I hope you never have to use it. This isn't Hollywood or a video game, this is real life and there are consequences, so be careful.

Something else to consider is how to carry your weapon. If you put the firearm somewhere that's hard to access, such as in a pack or something like that, it could be a problem. It should be somewhere easy for you to access.

Chapter 22

Communication

One of the biggest single issues in these situations is going to be communication. How do I get in touch with someone in case of an emergency? This type of thing happens more than you think. Getting lost or injured in the wilderness is not a good thing to experience. Having some source of communication in situations like these is not only reassuring but also has a calming factor. We touched on this in previous chapters discussing new technologies such as satellite link devices.

Initially, I had no intentions to write much about these since I really don't have a lot of knowledge on them, but after quite a bit of research on these items, my curiosity of the products has grown tremendously. However, these are just my own opinions and I'm relaying that information to you folks.

The biggest thing with these satellite link devices is knowing how to use them properly, and I am sure it takes a lot of practice to familiarize yourself with all the functions that they provide. My suggestion is to get out and use it to learn everything, basically taking "baby steps" in the process, before you wander off into the woods somewhere.

There are several manufacturers of these products and I'm sure they all have their "claim to fame," but after doing the research, one of the most important features to have would be the SOS button. This is the one button you have to push in an emergency situation to send out the calvary. However, pushing this button does not mean rescue is instant. Basically, this initiates a chain of events to get the procedure underway. Another plus is the GPS type that allows you to track yourself going in, then you have a path to follow on the way out, and right back to where you started.

During my research of devices, I have learned a lot about these items. They do not all operate off of the same satellites. Actually, there are different organizations with their own satellites up there, orbiting the earth alongside government satellites, which are doing the same thing. Some offer the ability to actually have a two-way text conversation with a keypad, or via your cell phone, others may lack this function. Some can be programmed to send your location at a set interval, so it will at least let someone know you are still mobile and can track your progress.

Personally, if I were to purchase one of these, I would prefer one that has the ability to have two-way communication. The reason being, you would have the advantage to exchange important information, such as, "I am lost," or "I am injured". Also, with two-way communication, you can get updates on the response times and other important messages. These could also be used to help other people as well. If another person is out fishing and got hurt somehow, you could use it to get help for them as well.

Some of the downfalls of these devices are battery life for one. Some claim to have several hours of battery life, but you must consider what conditions these were tested under. Is the battery life going to be the same out in an open field as it would be deep in the woods? How waterproof *are* they? I mean, you are going fishing, and where do fish live? In the water of course. As I said before, some work via your cell phone, so there is another battery you have to worry about draining. Also, much like a cell phone's signal, there are going to be some areas you just do not have coverage.

If you do, consider buying one of these. Be prepared, because there are several different manufacturers with a lot of different "bells and whistles" to choose from. Just like buying a car, and like anything else—the more options you have, the more the price goes up.

I will say, if you are a guide, this would be a good investment for you and your business. Whether you are in locations that are easy to access or locations that require a hike, they could be beneficial to you and or your clients in an emergency situation.

Even if you do have one of these devices, you should still have a backup plan. Remember, let people know where you are going and when you intend to be back. Most cell phones have a location-sharing service that you can share with friends and family members. Even if you do get out of cell service it will report your last location with a timestamp. This can give rescue workers a general idea of the area you're in, if need be.

I have spoken with a few different people who actually have these types of devices and use them on a regular basis. They seemed to be very pleased and were able to answer a lot of my questions. One person I spoke with told me he has actually used them throughout the Smoky Mountain National Park, several trips out in the Western states, and said he never experienced a problem with signal loss.

If you fish in the backwoods or if you fish ten feet from the parking lot, it's still a good idea to have something just in case. Especially if you have a serious medical condition. Remember, in medical emergency situations—time is of the essence!

If you are like me—not tech-savvy—and you decide to purchase one, you may want to find someone to teach you how to use it properly. However, all the ones I've looked at seem to have figured out how to make the emergency button "idiot proof," ensuring you do not accidentally hit it.

On a lot of these devices, people can track your every movement if you give them the proper permission to do so. They can even track how long you spend at each spot. This can be a good thing but may also be a problem.

Now, this never happened to me. But this happened to a friend of mine, who will remain nameless. If you tell your significant other you are going fishing and they decide to look at the computer to see where you are on the creek, only to find out you are not on the creek, but at a place called Knockers on the Lake—chances are they won't be too happy. When you come home and they ask how the fishing went, and mention something about Knocker's on the Lake, you'll know you've been caught! You can't deny it either, because not only is it right there on the computer screen but they'll see how long you were there too. Then they check the banking account and find out how much money you withdrew at the ATM—conveniently located inside a place called Knocker's on the Lake! Then, guess what happens? Every time you want to go fishing, *that* is going to come up! You know why? Because they never forget!

Chapter 23

"Hey, What Is That Guy Doing in the Water?"

I decided to add this in the book after watching a fishing video online. Two guys are in a raft on a river somewhere. One is rowing and the other fishing and a camera running, of course. While they are making their way downriver, all of a sudden, you see another guy floating downstream in the water. Luckily for him, he was wearing a life jacket! Anyway, the expressions on their faces when they see the person floating by were reminiscent of, "Hey, what is that guy doing in the water?"

Well, to make a long story short, they rescue the guy, and he is able to get back to his boat and everyone lives happily ever after. Another thing I noticed was everyone remained calm, and it made for a much better situation.

Have you ever thought about this? If so, have you ever thought about what you would do, and how you would do it? Fortunately, the man that was in the river, did two things to help himself. One, he had on his life jacket. The second thing he did was remain calm. Folks, I cannot stress to you how important it is that in a situation like this, you must do your best to remain calm.

In a panic situation, your blood pressure goes up along with your breathing rate, which may lead to hyperventilation. On top of all that, you may begin to experience dizziness and tingling at your fingertips. Then, the next thing that may happen is confusion. We can't leave that out. So, if you have not figured it out yet, your day is just getting worse here!

Now with all that being said, consider having to deal with someone in this situation. So, if you are in a situation where you are going to try and help or even rescue a person in distress and they are in full-blown panic mode.

You must do your best to remain calm. If you start to freak out, things are going to go downhill fast. The person you are trying to help notices you are calm; they may actually begin to calm down. Regardless, you need to keep a level head. After thirty-three years in the fire service, I saw some people in some bad situations. I saw stuff that made me want to throw up or scared the hell out of me. But having a patient involved, I had to put on a good poker face because I knew if I lost it, then the patient was going to lose it too, and the situation was going to go downhill fast.

If you are a guide, and you do float trips, something you should consider carrying in your boat is called a throw bag. Now, if you are not familiar with a throw bag, it is something widely used in Swiftwater Rescue situations. A throw bag is pretty much what it sounds like. It is a small bag with fifty to eighty-five feet of rope in it, preferably some type of floating rope, and a color that is highly visible. The bag itself should be a highly visible color as well and made from a polypropylene material to make the bag float as well.

The nice thing about a throw bag is it keeps all the rope contained in the bag, so it does not get scattered out and underfoot, or tangled on anything lying around in the boat. Basically, the way these are deployed, you hold onto the loose end of the rope and toss the bag toward the person in the water. When you toss it in their direction, the rest of the rope plays out of the bag. The end of the rope is threaded through the bottom of the bag, so it does not come loose from the rope. Of course, the key here is to land it within reach of the person in the water. With practice, you can become a pretty accurate thrower.

Now you may be thinking—*throw bag?* Why not go in the water after them? The reason you want to avoid this is because the person you are trying to help may be a danger to you. Especially if the person is not wearing a PFD. They could be in full-blown panic mode, and their actions may be very unpredictable. The results could end up drowning both of you. This is a very dangerous situation.

Fortunately, the person handling the boat in the video did an excellent job in maneuvering the boat and pulling up to the person in the water, while the other person was retrieving the potential drowning victim out of the water, and into the boat to safety. This could have gone very differently but fortunately, everyone remained calm.

Chapter 24

Debris and Obstacles in the Water

We have gone over this in previous chapters already. Most debris or other obstacles you may encounter are usually from Mother Nature. Natural items such as tree branches, limbs, rocks, and such. However, occasionally you may encounter something of the man-made variety. You see, humans have not always been good stewards of the land, and even today we still do not have 100 percent participation in this process, but I will say, it has improved a lot over the years. There are different organizations now that focus on the well-being of our streams, and the health of the streams seems to be improving tremendously. At one time in our history, creeks and rivers—even oceans—have been dumping grounds for all types of debris and in some places, even chemicals. Honestly, it was a combination of ignorance and carelessness. People seemed to have the thought process of—*"Throw it in the water, and don't worry about it."*

This thought process created some extremely bad situations. An example of this situation was the Cuyahoga River in Cleveland, Ohio. Believe it or not, this river was so polluted, it actually caught on fire, several times! If you do your research, you will find this has happened in other rivers as well. While this is an extreme example, I hope you'll never have to worry about anything like this happening. However, if you were to encounter a river of fire somewhere, then it is probably going to be something Biblical, probably from the book of Revelations, and I would suggest you drop to your knees and start praying!

In my experience, while fishing streams in more urban areas I have encountered large chunks of concrete in the water. It may have been from an old dam or bridge. Along with concrete comes something called rebar, which are steel bars within the concrete to reinforce the structure it once was. One problem with this is the rebar can protrude out from the broken concrete slabs, and this can wreak havoc not only on your waders, but your flesh as well. If you encounter something like this, the best thing to do is just avoid it altogether. There may be some great fishing there, but it is not worth getting hurt. Another thing to consider is that the concrete slabs may not be stable, so if you were to try to stand on or near one, it may move and could possibly be an entrapment situation. Again, folks, just avoid places like this if you encounter it.

"Detroit Riprap." Believe it or not, in some areas of the country, like the "Detroit Riprap," someone had the big idea to help prevent the erosion of riverbanks by stacking crushed cars on the riverbank. To this day in some areas, you may encounter old cars stacked along the riverbanks. Oddly enough, it seems to have worked, but it probably wasn't the best thing to use. Thankfully in 1972, congress passed the Clean Water Act, and it put a halt to this practice.

Natural debris is organic and will usually become weaker and break down over time. Man-made debris is a bit more complicated, because it is made to last over time. Another form of debris could be treated wooden fence posts, which are usually associated with farmers' pastures and such along with sections of fence, or barbwire. One of the dangers with the fence and barbed wire is it can become lodged underwater, or in a bank, and become an entanglement that you could get caught up in, which can lead to a bad day. Also, rebar, fence, and barbed wire can also wreak havoc on your waders and flesh.

You also may encounter this *anywhere* on the stream, not just near a pasture. A section of it may have been washed away during a storm and ended up downstream somewhere.

I have also encountered old railroad crossties, most likely dumped in the water after they were replaced with new ones under the existing train tracks.

So how do we prevent these situations? Again, let me say, "Be aware of your surroundings!"

Chapter 25

Taking Out the Trash

All right, let's say you loan your car to a friend. After they bring it back, you back, you take a look at the car, and notice it looks like they used it in a dirt track race. Then you open it up and find out they left it full of gas—*but not gasoline.* Shortly after you recover from the sulfuric smell, you notice breakfast burrito wrappers inside on the floor! After letting it air out for a while, and you get in to dispose of the breakfast burrito wrappers, you notice the fuel gauge reads empty. They didn't have the common decency to fill it up!

Now, think about this—a landowner has one of the best streams in the area, crossing their property. Out of common decency, they allow you to fish on their property. So, you go down there and fish for a while, take a break, eat a pack of crackers, (Bet you thought I was going to say a breakfast burrito) and drink a soft drink. When you're done, you toss the can and the cellophane wrapper, and bottle over in the woods. What is the difference between this and what your buddy did when he borrowed your car? Nothing really. They are both negligent and downright disrespectful!

Folks, we need to be respectful of other people's property! I know it's not just us as fishermen; it is people in general. As well as fishing, I have encountered this while hiking and hunting.

Too many people have the mindset of just throwing their trash wherever they feel. Folks, this is very inconsiderate. The property owner allows you to fish on their property, so you should be a bit more respectful and do your best and keep it clean.

As I mentioned earlier in the book, I have been an outdoorsman all of my life. I have approached property owners several times to get permission—either to hunt or fish on their property. If they said yes, it was usually followed by "but don't leave any trash" or if they said no, it was usually because they have had bad experiences with other people leaving trash or damaging their property.

This is one of the reasons why good streams get posted as PRIVATE PROPERTY. The landowners simply get fed up with people being disrespectful, so they will go to the hardware store and invest in a few NO TRESPASSING signs.

If you haven't figured it out already, there is a remedy to this situation. Don't leave any trash, don't damage any property, be respectful to the landowner and their property.

Now, I have a suggestion for you to try. Take a plastic grocery bag and put it in a pocket of your waders, vest, or whatever type of pack you use. Then, when you run across a small piece of trash, pick it up, and put it away until you run across some more. This will work for small items, but for larger items, toss them up on the bank, so when you are leaving, you can stop and pick it up.

Depending on where you are fishing, some streams actually have trash cans nearby for you to dump your unwanted trash. That way you don't have to haul it all the way home with you. It never seems to fail—I will be within walking distance of one of these trash cans and find trash that someone else was too lazy to carry up there.

This is a simple process we all need to remember and participate in. Fish need clean water to survive. No clean water equals no fish, it's a simple equation.

Also, there are groups and organizations you can get involved with and volunteer at local and state levels to help out with "stream clean ups." The organizations thrive on volunteer power, and needless to say—the more the better. If you have a group of people you fish with, maybe all of you could get involved and help out.

If nothing else, you and some of your fishing buddies can take some time and go out to a stream to do a cleanup. I am sure the property owners will appreciate it.

If you are a child of the '70s like me, you will remember pull tabs on drink cans. People used to pull the tab off and throw it away. Well, according to research, the can manufacturers quit using these in 1975. I still find these occasionally in stream banks.

Stream Safety & Fly Fishing

Remains of an aluminum can that was probably made in the '70s or early '80s. It had a pull tab on the top. This was found in a creek bank in 2024.

Chapter 26

Get Your Mind Right

Hopefully everything you've read has given you some good ideas and preparation for a trip—be it a day, or a multi-day excursion. Not all of us have the luxury of living on a stream where we can walk out the door and fish. Most of us have to pack up our vehicle and be prepared for the day. It may be a short trip to the water, or it may be a few hours to the stream from where you live. With being away from your home base, it is a good idea to have a few supplies. I used to carry enough stuff for me and probably five or six other fishermen. Then I realized I could shed some of the stuff I don't use ever. However, that does not mean I leave the rest of the stuff at home. I purchased a small tote to put my extra items in, so when I plan to go fishing somewhere, the tote goes in the truck. I carry extra fly boxes, spare spools of tippet, leaders, bug spray, a few tools, WD-40, and of course duct tape—along with some other miscellaneous items. This box can be a trip saver because if I don't have it in my chest pack, I can go back to the truck and get it.

Something else that's always good to have is a towel and a change of clothes. At least pants, a shirt, and some socks. Having an extra set of clothes is always good in case you fall into the water. You need to try to avoid a hypothermia situation. As I mentioned earlier, if you fall into cold water, the wet clothes you have on are going to prevent your body from retaining its core temperature, so you need to get the wet clothes off, then dry yourself off, and get dry clothing on your body. Folks, this should be done as soon as possible, which means you may not have the luxury of doing this indoors, so you can't be shy about this. Just watch out for "Meat Gazers"!

Another thing. I've talked about electrical devices, such as flashlights, GPS, cell phones, and other items. Before you take off on your trip, be sure and check these things to make sure they have batteries in them. Or if they are rechargeable, be sure to make sure they have a full charge. Some extra batteries would also be a good idea.

A cooler is a must. You have got to have something to keep the beer cold . . .

Oops! I meant water. I really don't know how beer jumped out there. Ice will work, but I tend to prefer the freezable packs. Other than keeping the drinks cold, they can also be used in a medical emergency, such as a sprained ankle or possibly an insect bite or sting. Simply place the pack on the injured area to help keep any swelling down. If you don't care for the freezable packs, try to keep a zip lock bag handy so you can fill that with ice. Speaking of that, if you haven't done it lately, you might want to check your first aid kit to see if you need to replace any items.

Usually when I go out for just the day, I still carry some type of food, such as a fruit selection, crackers, or some granola bars. I also bring a bag to dispose of trash.

Before heading out, you should always tell someone where you are going, and how long you will be gone. Just in case.

Now, on the way to the stream, if I start getting down close to half a tank of fuel, I'm going to stop and top off the tank. The reason for this is, I may be forced to take a different route home and may not be familiar with the route. There may be a tree down across the road, an accident, or it could be a license check! So, to be on the safe side, I am going to make sure I have enough fuel to get back home.

Another thing I have a habit of doing while enroute to the stream is make mental notes when I pass a fire station, or rescue squad, or anything of the like, just in case.

Occasionally, you should check your mobile phone's signal strength and also try to make mental notes to see where it is the strongest as well as the weakest. Even if you fish the same stream all your life, you should do this because the signal strength may change due to atmospheric conditions, or after your phone gets to

be a few years old, and the carrier is trying to get you to invest in a new phone.

Before I step into the water, I get to the stream, I gear myself up with my waders and boots on, and my fly rod is all rigged up. Then I tend to do a survey of the area. I am not only seeing if I spot any fish, but I am also looking around for any hazards, such as downed trees, or debris of any kind. Occasionally, I'll look at the ground to see if I notice any animal tracks. Then, I look for the best place to enter the water. Once I find my starting point in the water, I will scan upstream, then downstream. Even while I am actively fishing—every few minutes—again, I will scan upstream, then downstream. Scan upstream is always watching for debris that may be floating downstream.

The downstream scan is part of being aware of my surroundings. Also, always try to remember where your means of egress are, just in case you need to exit the water in a hurry.

If you are downstream from a bridge, big rocks, downed trees, or any other obstructions protruding from the water, these items can catch and collect debris, but due to the continuous flow of the current, it can break loose at any time and begin to travel downstream, heading your direction.

I know this is a lot to do. You already are trying to watch where you cast to keep yourself from hooking a tree. Then watch your line and/or strike indicator in case a fish strikes. Then your Buddy is downstream, probably up to no good. Yeah, it's a lot to remember, but with a little practice, you will become proficient.

FYI, facing the current, you are looking upstream. If the *current is to your back,* then you are looking downstream. Now, facing downstream, the bank to your right is called "river right," and the bank to your left is "river Left." If you *turn and face upstream,* the bank to your right is still "river Left" and the bank to your left is still "river Right". This is done to avoid confusion in communications during emergency situations.

Notice the tree upstream on "river right" with the roots washed out and undercut. Also notice the limbs hanging over the water.
This tree is unstable and could fall at any time.

Signs of wildlife around the stream.

Chapter 27

In Closing

Before I made the decision to write this book, I paid a lot of attention to what other people were doing out on the streams (and I still do). Watching how they would navigate the streams, entering and exiting the water. I also talked with a lot of people about their experiences on the water—good and bad. Interestingly enough, most of the folks I spoke with really had never even thought about too many safety issues.

So, hopefully you got something from reading this book. Yes, it's a fair amount of information to go over. I have no intentions of scaring anyone away from the sport of fly Fishing. My intentions are to give people more preparation for a "just in case" situation. You may go all of your life and never experience a single issue during your times fishing, and I hope that everyone enjoys the sport. However, here in the real world, poo-poo happens. So, it's better to be prepared for it.

In all my years of the fire service we got all types of training. However, it seemed that the Swiftwater Rescue was something highly overlooked. I guess because at that time, we didn't really have that much call for it. And if we did, we usually just improvised and got lucky. Until an incident happened one night when a civilian decided to get on a small raft during a heavy rainstorm, and jump into a swollen creek, then ride it downstream. Now, I'm not sure if the words came out of his mouth before jumping in the water, "Hey Y'all, watch this!" But needless to say, it did not work out too well, and he ended up having to be rescued from the fast-moving water. And yes, he did survive his trip down the creek. Let's just say, it was not a smart move on his part.

Folks, if any of you out there are affiliated with a fire department—paid or volunteer—a rescue squad, any EMS, guides—if you haven't already, you should strongly consider taking a Swiftwater Rescue course. After all the training I've had in my thirty-three years in the fire service, I will say the Swiftwater Rescue course was some of the best training I've had. This class will make you respect the power of water and look at moving water totally differently than you do now.

I also highly recommend CPR and first aid training. Hopefully you will never have to use it, but it is good to know.

Things to always remember:

- Always be aware of your surroundings.
- Try not to panic if you do run into an alarming situation.
- Water does not get tired, but you will.
- Please don't leave trash behind.
- Don't spit into the wind.

Acknowledgments

There are a few people that I would like to mention:

First, my Mom. She cared nothing for fishing. She knew nothing about fishing, however she had 2 young boys who loved to go fishing, so whenever she could, we would all get in the car and ride out to my uncle's farm so my brother and I could spend the day fishing my Uncle's farm pond. Thanks Mom, I miss you!

To my friend and mentor Richard Griggs, owner of Carolina Mountain Sports in Statesville, North Carolina: You have taught me a lot about Fly Fishing and have become a great friend.

Another friend and mentor, Micky Reavis, fly tyer extraordinaire. Mickey is one of the best fly tyers around and thankfully he was patient enough to teach me the art of fly tying.

About the Author

G.R. Murphy (Murf) was born and raised in Charlotte, North Carolina, and grew up fishing, anywhere and everywhere, freshwater and saltwater. At the age of twenty-four, he joined the Charlotte Fire Department, where he also became an emergency medical technician as well as a swiftwater rescue technician. Now retired, he resides with his wife somewhere in the "Brushy Mountains" of North Carolina, fly fishing as much as possible.

www.ingramcontent.com/pod-product-compliance
Lightning Source LLC
Chambersburg PA
CBHW052144070526
44585CB00017B/1965